W9-CKL-817

GREAT DISCOVERIES IN SCIENCE

The Big Bang Theory

Rachel Keranen

Cavendish
Square
New York

Published in 2018 by Cavendish Square Publishing, LLC
243 5th Avenue, Suite 136, New York, NY 10016

Copyright © 2018 by Cavendish Square Publishing, LLC

First Edition

No part of this publication may be reproduced, stored in a retrieval system, or transmitted in any form or by any means—electronic, mechanical, photocopying, recording, or otherwise—without the prior permission of the copyright owner. Request for permission should be addressed to Permissions, Cavendish Square Publishing, 243 5th Avenue, Suite 136, New York, NY 10016. Tel (877) 980-4450; fax (877) 980-4454.

Website: cavendishsq.com

This publication represents the opinions and views of the author based on his or her personal experience, knowledge, and research. The information in this book serves as a general guide only. The author and publisher have used their best efforts in preparing this book and disclaim liability rising directly or indirectly from the use and application of this book.

CPSIA Compliance Information: Batch #CS17CSQ

All websites were available and accurate when this book was sent to press.

Library of Congress Cataloging-in-Publication Data

Names: Keranen, Rachel, author.
Title: The Big bang theory / Rachel Keranen.
Description: New York : Cavendish Square Publishing, [2018] | Series: Great discoveries in science | Includes bibliographical references and index.
Identifiers: LCCN 2016053663 (print) | LCCN 2016051293 (ebook) | ISBN 9781502627704 (library bound) | ISBN 9781502627711 (E-book)
Subjects: LCSH: Big bang theory--Juvenile literature. | Expanding universe--Juvenile literature. | Cosmogony--Juvenile literature.
Classification: LCC QB991.B54 (print) | LCC QB991.B54 K46 2018 (ebook) | DDC 523.1/8--dc23
LC record available at https://lccn.loc.gov/2016053663

Editorial Director: David McNamara
Editor: Caitlyn Miller
Copy Editor: Michele Suchomel-Casey
Associate Art Director: Amy Greenan
Designer: Lindsey Auten
Production Coordinator: Karol Szymczuk
Photo Research: J8 Media

The photographs in this book are used by permission and through the courtesy of: Cover HENNING DALHOFF/SPL/Getty Images; p. 4 MARK GARLICK/SPL/Getty Images; p. 8 Heritage Image Partnership Ltd/Alamy Stock Photo; p. 13 http://maps.bpl.org (http://www.flickr.com/people/24528911@N05)/Wikimedia Commons/File:Planisphaerium Ptolemaicum siue machina orbium mundi ex hypothesi Ptolemaica in plano disposita (2709983277).jpg/CC BY 2.0; p. 15 NYPL/Science Source/Getty Images; p. 17 Palomar/Radio-NSF/NRAO/VLA; p. 18 NASA/W. Liller/Wikimedia Commons/File:Lspn comet halley.jpg/Public Domain; p. 21 Adventtr/E+/Getty Images; p. 26 Art Directors/TRIP/Alamy Stock Photo; p. 29 Russell Kightley/Science Source; p. 32 Mmaxer/Shutterstock.com; p. 33 Designua/Shutterstock.com; p. 35 Dr Juerg Alean/Science Source; p. 39 BlueRingMedia/Shutterstock.com; p. 48 GL Archive/Alamy Stock Photo; p. 50 Topical Press Agency/Hulton Archive/Getty Images; p. 54 Roger Ressmeyer/Corbis/VCG/Getty Images; p. 58 Carl Iwasaki/The LIFE Images Collection/Getty Images; p. 63 NASA/Wikimedia Commons/File:Horn Antenna-in Holmdel, New Jersey.jpeg/Public Domain; p. 66 NASA; p. 70 Okili77/Shutterstock.com; p. 72 FT2/Wikimedia Commons/File:Massive star cutaway pre-collapse.png/Public Domain; p. 78 NASA/JPL-Caltech/ESA/Wikimedia Commons/File:PIA16874-CobeWmapPlanckComparison-20130321.jpg/Public Domain; p. 81 NASA/WMAP Science Team/Wikimedia Commons/File:CMB Timeline300 no WMAP.jpg/Public Domain; p. 83 Courtesy of V. Springel and the Virgo Consortium; p. 87 SCIENCE SOURCE/Getty Images; p. 92 Atlas Experiment © 2011 CERN; p. 95 ArSciMed/Science Source; p. 101 Peter Ginter/Science Faction/Getty Images; p. 103 Henze, NASA/Wikimedia Commons/File:This visualization shows what Einstein envisioned.jpg/Public Domain; p. 105 Detlev van Ravenswaay/Science Source.

Printed in the United States of America

Contents

In the birth of the universe, the
universe had an enormous energy
density and expanded rapidly.

Introduction: Cosmological Curiosity

Since the beginning of recorded human history, people have sought explanations for where we come from and why Earth and the sky are as they are.

Has the universe been this way forever? Did it have a moment of origin? What is it made of? What principles governed its shape and movement?

The study of the history and evolution of the universe is called **cosmology**. In the early years of human civilization, our ancestors' knowledge of the world was limited to their local environment, weather phenomena, and what they could observe in the sky with their own eyes. Their cosmologies described the separation of Earth and the sky, the creation of the first gods and men, and the formation of our planet as we see it today. These narratives were deeply mythological and depended on gods and supernatural phenomena to explain the creation and evolution of the world.

Over the course of millennia, the way these cosmologies were created evolved. As intellectual discourse grew in the academies of ancient Greece, now-famous philosophers set forth sweeping descriptions of the universe's structure and characteristics. However, while cosmology describes the evolution of the universe over time, the influential philosophers

Plato, Aristotle, and Ptolemy believed that the universe beyond Earth was perfect and unchanging.

After the Middle Ages, Europe underwent a period of artistic, cultural, and scientific innovation known as the Renaissance. From this surge of progress came the **Scientific Revolution**, an era in which old notions of perfection and stasis (lack of change) were broken down by scientists such as Nicolaus Copernicus, Galileo Galilei, Tycho Brahe, and Johannes Kepler. New methods for conducting science in a more observation-focused, testable manner grew as well.

Developments in optics and, subsequently, telescopes significantly aided astronomers in the Scientific Revolution and beyond. As telescopes grew in power and resolution, they played an increasingly significant role in shaping our cosmology throughout the 1800s up to modern day. So too did the advancements in understanding the properties of light and the **electromagnetic spectrum**, including the new field of spectroscopy discovered in the 1800s. With more ways to measure the light coming from outer space and the ability to garner information from that light, our ability to learn about deep space accelerated.

In the early 1900s, Edwin Hubble discovered that there are galaxies beyond our own. When the physicist Albert Einstein introduced his theory of general relativity, it raised big questions about the history of the universe. Was it expanding? Was it contracting? And if it was changing, what was it like in the past?

Though many scientists had preferred models of an unchanging universe because considering a moment of creation came too near religious narratives, twentieth-century scientists were forced to consider the possibility that the universe had a finite age and was changing over time.

The physicist Georges Lemaître proposed an expansion model of the universe that began with the decay of a primordial "super atom." Though originally ignored or scorned by other physicists, another discovery by Hubble showed that the universe really was expanding over time. This finding had a clear implication: if galaxies are moving apart, they must at one point have been closer. Using the speed at which galaxies were receding, astronomers could calculate a time at which all galaxies were in one small, dense region of space.

That small, dense region was perhaps not exactly the super atom Lemaître had proposed, but it spurred astronomers onward to discover just what did happen at that time.

In the late 1940s, George Gamow and Ralph Alpher proposed a new version of the big bang theory, as it later came to be called. Gamow and Alpher suggested that the universe began in a dense, highly energetic state from which elements (and thus matter) formed. Discoveries through the following decades lent more details, as well as some major revisions, to the big bang theory, but that basic premise stands: according to the standard model of cosmology, the universe began 13.8 billion years ago in a highly concentrated region of space that underwent rapid inflationary expansion.

Though the big bang model of cosmology is accepted as the standard model, there is still much to learn about the beginning of our universe. Physicists are studying the formation of matter and **antimatter**; the early, rapid inflation of the universe; and the mysterious **dark matter** that shaped the stars and galaxies we know today. Others are looking at whether our universe is the only universe out there. The big bang is an exhilarating theory of the beginning of our universe, and scientists are continuously looking for more details and supporting evidence.

In Maori mythology, Rangi (sky) and Papa (Earth) were intertwined until their son Tane, god of the forest, forced them apart.

CHAPTER 1

How Did the Universe Begin?

"All men by nature desire to know."

—Aristotle

The science of the universe and how it has developed over time is called cosmology. Throughout history, humans have asked cosmological questions. How did Earth form? How did the universe form? What forces have shaped the universe over time? In the early days of human civilization, in lieu of science and technology, different civilizations created their own answers to those questions.

At the beginning of human history, observational data was limited to a group's local environment and what they could see of the sky with the naked eye. From these observations, cultures created mythological explanations for how Earth, the sky, and humans came to be. Looking back, these mythologies can seem entertaining but implausible. However, in early human history, science and mathematics were rudimentary and technology was limited.

As the role of science and mathematics grew in human culture, the study of the universe became increasingly scientific and cosmological. Over the last few centuries, scientists have relied more and more on an observation-based scientific method, documenting observable phenomena and coming up with testable hypotheses for those phenomena.

MYTHOLOGIES

"Before there was any light there was only darkness, all was night. Before there was even darkness there was nothing."

These sentences, taken from a myth from the Maori people in New Zealand, describe the very beginning of the universe.

From the nothingness and the darkness, the story proceeds as follows:

The universe grew and produced Rangi (heaven) and Papa (Earth), a husband and wife pair intertwined in a close embrace. Rangi and Papa had many sons who lived in the darkness between their parents' bodies and schemed to kill their parents. One son, Tawhiri (the god of wind and storm), advocated for separation instead and so Tane-mahuta (the god of the forest) pressed Rangi and Papa—sky and Earth—apart.

In the Christian creation story, there is a similar void until the creator, God, says, "Let there be light." God continues to create the sky, waters, and Earth, followed by plants, celestial objects, animals, and eventually the first man and woman.

In Shinto, the indigenous religion in Japan, heaven and Earth separated out of chaos. Earth was initially formless until the brother and sister gods Izanagi and Izanami appeared and were tasked with creating structure. Together, the pair created the islands that formed the Japanese archipelago. The pair also gave birth to numerous other deities, including the god of fire, the sun goddess, the moon god, and the storm god.

Images of primordial chaos, darkness, and light permeate mythologies across the world, from the Maori mythologies to the biblical book of Genesis to Shinto and beyond. These creation myths (and many others) put forth lineages of gods and humans and other worldly creatures that give shape to

Earth until it looks like the land we know today, filled with humans, plants, and animals.

These examples are just a few among a vast array of mythologies that have shaped cultures across the world.

In the academic definition of the word, a mythology is a powerful narrative that is considered to be of great importance, is recited at special occasions, and explains how and why the world has come to be as it is today. Mythologies contain meaning and truth for the groups of people that recite and maintain them, but they may not have meaning or truth for other groups of people.

Therein lies the difference between mythologies and science. Modern science seeks to find theories and laws that hold true, no matter who performs the experiment. Science seeks objective explanations for natural phenomena rather than subjective narratives.

The scientific method as we know it wouldn't emerge as a dominant method until the Scientific Revolution. In the meantime, the ancient Greeks laid the foundation for much of Western science, philosophy, and cosmology.

The ANCIENT GREEKS

The ancient Greek philosophers, scientists, and mathematicians were extremely influential in the Western world for millennia after their time.

In 387 BCE, Greek philosopher Plato founded the first institution of higher learning in the Western world. Plato and other Greek philosophers emphasized an intellectual approach to cosmology and other sciences that used evidence, reason, and debate to come to conclusions about the universe.

Yet Plato believed that knowledge was best gained from reasoning, not through observation. Plato divided the universe into two categories: the physical, visible world and

Ancient Chronologies

Many ancient cultures observed the cyclical nature of things, from human life and death to the return of each season to the phases of the moon. Influenced by these rhythms, they created cyclical chronologies of the great cosmos.

The ancient Mayans, for example, as well as the Aztecs and Incas, believed in eternal cycles of life, death, and rebirth. They believed that the smaller cycles, such as the phases of the moon, were part of a larger cycle of the universe. The ancient Babylonians believed in a cosmic cycle made of 600 *saros* that were 3,600 years each, for a total of 2,160,000 years before the world recreated itself.

Similarly, in the writing *Huang Chi Ching Shih* by Shao K'ang-chieh in the Sung dynasty (960–1279 CE), Shao describes a cosmic timeline called the *yuan* that consists of twelve periods (*hui*) of 10,800 years each. Over the course of the cosmic cycle, the world improves and then declines. After a full yuan, 129,600 years in total, heaven and Earth end and are born again. The cycle repeats into eternity.

There was no way to determine if these large, repeating cycles were accurate, but they served at least one purpose: death was not so final if all was born again, and again, and again into eternity.

This artistic rendering, while more of a zodiac than a Ptolemaic model, is a beautifully crafted Earth-centered system.

the world of "Forms." According to Plato, the Forms, though nonphysical, are the most accurate reality. He believed we can gain knowledge from them through deductive reasoning. The material world, Plato believed, is imperfect and therefore not a good source of knowledge.

Plato's student Aristotle disagreed with this element of Plato's approach and placed more emphasis on observation of the natural world. Aristotle created a model of the universe with Earth fixed at the center and the planets, sun, and stars moving around it in nested crystalline spheres.

This model was added to and refined by Ptolemy, an influential astronomer, mathematician, and geographer of Greek descent born in Egypt.

In 150 CE, Ptolemy published a new geocentric model of the universe that attempted to make Aristotle's perfectly spherical model fit with the observed irregular motion of celestial bodies. Ptolemy added several mechanisms including an epicycle, which was a smaller orbit each planet makes in the course of orbiting Earth. Though incorrect, the Ptolemaic model of the universe predicted celestial motion relatively accurately and was used for over a millennium by European and Islamic astronomers.

In retrospect, the ancient Greeks were far from accurate in their cosmologies and models of the universe. However, their work was vastly different from ancient mythologies. The Greeks had their gods, but in their sciences they emphasized rational thought and mathematics.

The Greeks were limited by their desire to find perfection and mathematical harmony in the universe, but they moved the cosmological discussion from mythology to mathematics, nature, and rationalism. They believed that nature is knowable and understandable rather than under the control of supernatural beings.

The SCIENTIFIC REVOLUTION

After the contributions of the ancient Greeks, science in Europe moved forward relatively slowly, especially during the Middle Ages.

The Middle Ages in Europe began with the fall of the Roman Empire in the fifth century CE and lasted until somewhere between the thirteenth and fifteenth centuries, depending on the region of Europe.

The Middle Ages were characterized by a general decline in quality of life after the fall of the Roman civilization. The Roman Catholic Church was the major social and political force, and it dominated the intellectual sphere.

From the eighth to the fourteenth centuries, many of the advancements in astronomy and mathematics took place in the Islamic world, centered around an academy called the House of Wisdom in Baghdad. There, the motivation for better astronomy and the required geometry came from the desire to accurately observe Islamic holy days, which follow a lunar calendar.

In about the twelfth century, conditions began to change in Europe. Travel and communication became faster and safer. City-states emerged in Italy; national monarchies formed in France, England, and Spain; and secular (nonreligious) education became more common. Agricultural developments made it possible for lower classes to enjoy a balanced diet, and the population grew rapidly. As the Middle Ages ended, Europe entered a period known as the **European Renaissance**, or the "rebirth" of European civilization.

During this time period, the cultural decline of the Middle Ages reversed and art, scholarship, innovation, and commerce flourished. Leonardo da Vinci painted the *Mona Lisa*, European explorers set sail for far-off continents, and Johannes Gutenberg invented the printing press. The printing press had an enormous impact on education and scholarship as it led to the mass production of printed books and, consequently, the spread of information and ideas. From this flourishing of arts and sciences of the Renaissance grew a period called the Scientific Revolution.

Heliocentrism Surges

In 1543, the Polish mathematician and astronomer Nicolaus Copernicus published *De revolutionibus orbium coelestium* (*On the Revolutions of the Heavenly Spheres*). The text was largely a mathematical work, but it also contained a heliocentric (sun-centered) model of the planetary system.

It should be noted that Copernicus was not the first to propose a heliocentric model of the universe. The ancient Greek Aristarchus had proposed a heliocentric model in the third century BCE, as had the Indian mathematician and astronomer Aryabhata in 490 CE. However, Copernicus's work came right at the beginning of a massive shift in

Western science and was an influential text for many subsequent scientists.

De revolutionibus outlined a simple theory that accounted for the movement of the planets and placed the planets in order from Mercury outward. Though his model was a significant improvement in terms of arrangement, Copernicus still believed in perfectly circular orbits and therefore calculations based on his model had many flaws. At first, few scientists paid much attention to the book's heliocentric theory at all, for it simply did not fit into the Aristotelian way of thinking that still dominated Western science. Over time, however, as the physical sciences grew, *De revolutionibus* would find its place in the prevailing scientific view.

A Changing Universe

In the 1570s, the Danish astronomer Tycho Brahe observed two celestial phenomena that helped show that the universe was neither unchanging nor divided into an imperfect earthly realm and a perfect, impenetrable heavenly realm.

Brahe's first observation was of a **supernova** in 1572 that shone brightly for about eighteen months. When a massive star reaches the end of its lifecycle, it dies in a brilliant supernova explosion. Though the explosion itself happens in about one hundred seconds, the peak brightness can last for several months.

At the time, astronomers did not know the true nature of supernovas, and Brahe mistook the phenomenon as the birth of a new star. Though Brahe was incorrect about the life cycle event he was observing, he correctly noted that the event took place among the stars.

Using the supernova's **parallax**, Brahe was able to calculate where the supernova had occurred. Parallax is the difference in an object's apparent position when viewed from two different

Copernicus dedicated *De revolutionibus* to Pope Paul III, but the church placed it on the forbidden books list decades later.

lines of sight. (You can observe parallax yourself by closing one eye, looking at an object, and then looking at the same object with just the other eye closed.) The apparent difference is greater when objects are closer, which means that parallax can be used to determine the distance to **comets**, stars, and other celestial objects.

In the fall of 1577, Brahe made his second significant observation when he observed a comet that passed near Earth.

Comets are often described as dirty snowballs. More specifically, comets are small bodies of rock, ice (including ices of water, carbon dioxide, ammonia, and methane), and dust that orbit the sun. In their orbits, comets typically travel both very far from and very near to the sun. The center of a comet is surrounded by a large cloud of gas and dust called the coma, which is created as the ice at the center of the comet is heated and sublimated by the sun. Material streams out of the coma as

The earliest recorded supernova took place in 185 CE and was documented by Chinese astronomers.

Some comets orbit the sun on predictable schedules, such as Halley's Comet, which passes by Earth about every seventy-five years.

the comet moves, creating a luminescent tail that can be up to tens of millions of kilometers long.

In Brahe's day, when comets came and went, scientists and philosophers thought that they must move beneath the moon in the imperfect and changing earthly realm. Aristotle himself had taught that comets, like lightning and meteors, occurred in Earth's atmosphere. At the time, comets were also often believed to be bad omens that preceded major disasters such as plagues and floods.

Brahe's calculations using parallax, however, showed that comets passed by far above Earth's atmosphere.

"I conclude that it was in the sphere of Venus," Brahe wrote in a 1578 manuscript. His measurements were not entirely accurate, but the implications were significant: if a comet was passing through the sky near Venus and then disappearing, not only were changes occurring in the celestial realm but also between Aristotle's theoretical crystalline spheres.

Brahe had already suspected that Aristotle's view of the universe was incorrect, and along with the supernova of 1572, his observations of the comet of 1577 suggested Brahe was right.

Though influential, not all of Brahe's astronomical ideas were correct, including his model of the universe. Brahe proposed a hybrid of the Ptolemaic and Copernican systems in which the sun, moon, and stars orbited Earth while the known planets revolved around the sun. Mathematically, Brahe's system was equal to Copernicus's model of a perfectly spherical heliocentric system (which also had its flaws), but it was fundamentally inaccurate.

It was Brahe's student Johannes Kepler who, after Brahe's death, brought about the next significant advancements in determining the structure of the universe.

An Imperfect Universe

Kepler began his degree at the University of Tübingen in Germany in 1589 and studied under a mathematics professor, Michael Maestlin, who was an adherent to the Copernican system. Maestlin lent Kepler *De revolutionibus*, which Kepler sensed was correct. He decided that he would demonstrate it was so.

In 1600, Kepler moved to Prague to assist Brahe, who at this point was serving as the imperial mathematician for Holy Roman Emperor Rudolph II. Over decades of work and with instruments he had designed, Brahe had created an enormous data set of astronomical observations. Kepler's task was to calculate planetary orbits from these observations.

When Brahe died in 1601, Kepler succeeded him as imperial mathematician to the emperor and inherited Brahe's data. With the intellectual freedom granted by imperial court life and Brahe's exceptionally accurate data, Kepler was able to determine that Mars moves in an elliptical orbit.

Kepler's second law tells us that planets move faster when near the sun and slower when farther away.

Kepler published his findings on the orbit of Mars in 1609 in a book called *Astronomia nova* (*New Astronomy*). It marked the introduction of Kepler's first law of planetary motion, which states that the planets move in elliptical orbits with the sun at one focus. (That is, the sun is located off from the center of the elliptical path.)

Also in 1609, the famous Italian astronomer Galileo Galilei built his first telescope. Over the next few years, Galileo made a multitude of discoveries, including the craggy surface of the moon, the four largest moons of Jupiter, and the phases of Venus.

The first observation showed that the moon's surface was as imperfect as Earth's surface. The discovery of Jupiter's moons showed that Earth was not the only body to have a satellite. (Galileo at first thought that the bright objects he saw were "fixed stars," but after observing them over time, he saw that they moved around, behind, and in front of Jupiter.) His observations of the phases of Venus showed that, with respect to Earth, Venus was sometimes on the far side of the sun and sometimes on the near side of the sun. In other words, Venus orbited the sun, not Earth.

The moon's irregularities and the discovery of Jupiter's moons were not part of the Aristotelian and Ptolemaic models of the universe, and Venus's orbit was simply not possible in the Aristotelian and Ptolemaic models.

In 1610, almost seventy years after Copernicus published *De revolutionibus*, Galileo published these observations and conclusions in a treatise (or pamphlet) titled *Sidereus Nuncius* (*Starry Messenger*). The first page read, with great fanfare and enthusiastic capitalization:

The Herald of the Stars unfolding GREAT and HIGHLY ADMIRABLE sights, and presenting to the gaze of everyone, but especially PHILOSPHERS,

and ASTRONOMERS, those things observed by
GALILEO GALILEI, Patrician of Florence, Public
Mathematician of the University of Padua, with the aid
of a TELESCOPE …

Sidereus Nuncius referred to the motion of Mercury, Venus,
and Mars around the sun and clearly promoted the Copernican
heliocentric model. The Catholic Church had deemed that
heliocentrism was heretical and ordered Galileo to avoid
teaching or defending heliocentrism in the future.

In 1633, however, after Galileo printed an implicit defense
of heliocentrism in *Dialogue Concerning the Two Chief World
Systems,* he was charged with heresy and sentenced to house
arrest for the remainder of his life. Though deemed a heretic,
Galileo succeeded in popularizing the Copernican system.

The developments that occurred during the Scientific
Revolution forever changed the way scientists, scholars, and
common people understood astronomy and cosmology. The
Aristotelian model had fallen. The universe was imperfect and
changing, and Earth was just one of many planets orbiting the
sun on elliptical paths.

The Scientific Method

The Scientific Revolution didn't just bring new knowledge and
discoveries—it also popularized the modern methodology
for scientific research, which would play an important role in
developing the prevailing modern cosmological theories.

Today, students in science classes across the world learn
the scientific method as a standard element of conducting an
experiment. The scientific method was not always a part of
how intellectuals arrived at conclusions, however, as shown by

the intellectual thought of the ancient Greek philosophers and church-influenced scholarship prior to the Scientific Revolution.

In general, the scientific method starts with the specific (an observation) and moves toward a more general principle (a theory that can explain observations). The tests must be replicable and, if subsequent tests show that a hypothesis does not hold true, the theory must be modified or thrown out entirely.

If analysis of test data shows the predictions are inaccurate, then the scientist must modify his or her hypothesis, make new predictions, and run more tests. When significant data shows that the predictions are accurate, the scientist can develop the hypothesis into a general theory.

During the Scientific Revolution, this focus on methodical observation, experiments, and inductive reasoning (finding general laws from particular instances) became the dominant scientific methodology. As scientists such as Galileo and Kepler focused on making observations over time and making conclusions based on large amounts of data, the pace of scientific discoveries accelerated and our knowledge of the universe began to expand rapidly.

From Mythology to Scientific Cosmology

Humans began making sense of the world around them through myths that told the story of creation. These myths were important to the cultures that created them, but they varied between societies. Today, we investigate the universe in a very different way.

Over the seventeenth, eighteenth, and nineteenth centuries, science and technology accelerated at breakneck pace, transforming, industrializing, and modernizing the world. There were developments in astronomy and physics, and scientists made huge advancements in their understanding of the scale of the universe and the movement of celestial bodies. These developments made way for a more scientific variation of the cosmological question: From a perspective embedded in the physical sciences and the scientific method, how did the universe come to be as it is today?

Before scientists could derive the big bang theory, the modern standard cosmological model, they needed specific advancements in science and technology. Our modern cosmology grew from a deeper understanding of optics, chemistry, and light, which we will explore in the next chapter.

Galileo was also interested in the laws of motion and discovered properties of falling objects and the trajectory of projectiles.

GALILEO.

CHAPTER 2

The Science of the Big Bang

Before the Scientific Revolution, there were significant knowledge gaps and technological barriers to understanding the first moments of the universe. Understanding the universe's early history required telescopes and spectroscopes, among other equipment. It required a nuanced understanding of the properties of light, chemical elements, and atoms. It required a dramatic twentieth-century revision of the scope of the universe. All of these scientific elements came together when Albert Einstein proposed a new theory of gravity that raised curious questions about the future—and past—of the universe.

OPTICS

When you look up at the sky at night with your unaided eye, you can see a beautiful array of stars and constellations. Without a telescope, it's hard to garner any information from those stars beyond their position in the night sky and their relative brightness. A crucial precursor to the invention of the telescope was the invention of the glass lens within it that created the necessary magnifying effect.

Lenses

Glass lenses as we know them today were first introduced toward the end of the thirteenth century. Glasswork had long been a tradition in places including Venice and Florence, and by the thirteenth century, craftsmen were producing small disks of glass that could correct the weakening vision of the elderly. The disks were convex on both sides, like a lentil, and were given the name "lentils of glass," or *lenses* in Latin. Soon, there were also concave lenses for correcting myopia, or nearsightedness.

The Refracting Telescope

The first telescope was invented in the Netherlands in the early 1600s. In the fall of 1608, two men independently filed patent applications for a telescope design. The first was Hans Lippershey, a German spectacle maker living in Middleburg, the Netherlands. Lippershey had invented a device through which "all things at a very great distance can be seen as if they were nearby."

A few weeks later, another Dutch spectacle maker, Jacob Metius, filed a patent for a device used for "seeing faraway things as though nearby." The Dutch States General in The Hague ultimately did not award patents to either of the men as the device was too easy to copy, but both men profited from their designs. Years later, a third Dutch spectacle maker named Zacharias Janssen claimed to have invented the first telescope.

The three Dutch inventors were all craftsmen, not astronomers. It was Galileo, the Italian astronomer, physicist, mathematician, and inventor, who first made the telescope famous.

Without having ever seen a telescope before, Galileo built a telescope in 1609 that used a convex lens at the end (called an objective lens) and a concave lens for the eyepiece. This first telescope made objects appear nine times larger than when viewed with the naked eye.

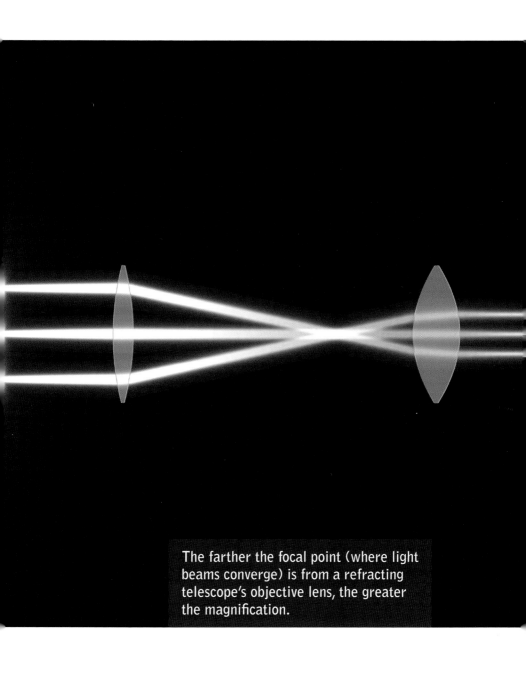

The farther the focal point (where light beams converge) is from a refracting telescope's objective lens, the greater the magnification.

After improving his telescope design, Galileo made many significant discoveries, including sunspots, four of Jupiter's moons, and "nebular patches" that he determined were actually regions filled with stars. And yet, the telescope Galileo used for these observations only made objects appear about thirty times closer and had a very small field of view (about a quarter of the full moon could be observed at a time).

These first astronomical telescopes were refracting telescopes, or telescopes that used lenses to bend light. In a refracting telescope, the light from celestial objects first passes through a lens at the end of the telescope, through a focal plane inside the telescope, and then through a second lens (the eyepiece lens) that enables the observer to view the magnified image. A major limitation of refracting telescopes is that different wavelengths of light bend at different angles when they pass through the glass lenses, and the resulting magnified image is slightly distorted. Over the next few centuries, telescope technology advanced significantly.

The Reflecting Telescope

The reflecting telescope, first built in 1668 by the English physicist Sir Isaac Newton, helped remedy the distortion of refracting telescopes. Reflecting telescopes use a concave mirror to reflect light instead of glass lenses that refract light. While different wavelengths of light refract at different angles, they do not disperse at different angles when reflected. Thus, a reflecting telescope has greater focus than a refracting telescope. Reflecting telescopes also don't require as long of domes as refracting telescopes, which makes them more economical and simple to construct.

Today, most telescopes are reflecting telescopes that use concave mirrors to reflect light. Larger mirrors can gather more light, and mirrors have grown in size over time. Today, the largest telescopes, such as the telescope at the Keck Observatory in Hawaii, use telescopes with multiple mirrors to produce the effect of a larger mirror at a lower cost.

LIGHT

Light permeates and illuminates our daily lives, but it also has the power to reveal vast amounts of information about the cosmos.

Knowing the speed of light, the different types of light, and what light spectra can tell us has been essential to studying the beginnings of the universe.

The Speed of Light

The speed of light is a significant metric in cosmology because when we know how fast light travels, we can use that speed in calculations of how far away different stars, galaxies, **nebulae** (clouds of gas and dust), and other phenomena are.

Aristotle thought that light traveled instantly, but today we know that light does have a finite speed. The first person to measure the speed of light with relative accuracy was the Danish astronomer Ole Römer in 1676. Römer had studied Jupiter's moon Io (discovered a half century earlier by Galileo), which is regularly eclipsed by Jupiter as Io moves behind Jupiter in its orbit. Sometimes, the eclipse happened sooner than expected or later than expected.

Römer realized that the early or late appearance of Io from behind Jupiter was due to the varying distance between Earth and Jupiter. When Earth was farther away from Jupiter, the light had to travel farther and thus arrived at Earth later than astronomers had expected. Though Io's orbit around Jupiter is regular, the timing of the eclipse varied by about an

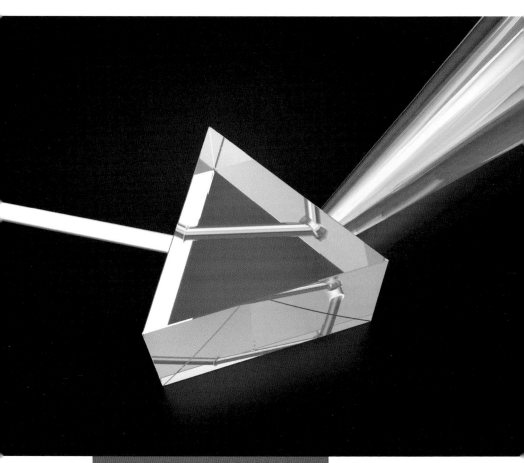

White light is composed of different wavelengths of light that refract at different angles when passing through a prism.

hour throughout the year due to the varying distance between the two planets. Römer estimated that the speed of light was 186,000 miles per second (299,344 km/s), which isn't far off from its modern-day measurement of 186,282 miles per second (299,792 km/s).

Visible Light Spectra

Another misconception of light was that it was a pure, white substance. As far back as Aristotle, scientists had believed that light creates a rainbow when passed through a prism because the light itself is modified.

In 1665, Isaac Newton proved differently with a simple but convincing experiment. On a sunny day at Cambridge University, Newton darkened his room and made a small hole in the shutter for a beam of light to pass through. Newton

THE ELECTROMAGNETIC SPECTRUM

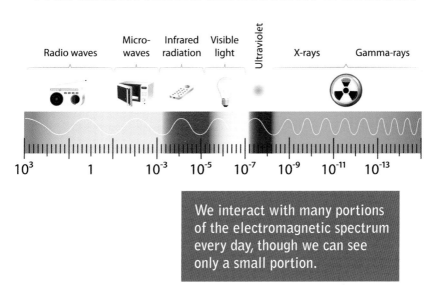

We interact with many portions of the electromagnetic spectrum every day, though we can see only a small portion.

placed a glass prism in the beam of light, creating a rainbow or light spectrum.

Newton then took a second prism and placed it upside down in front of the first prism. The spectrum of light, with all of its component colors, passed through the second prism and combined back into white light. In this way, Newton showed that white light contains all of the colors of the rainbow.

The Electromagnetic Spectrum

In the nineteenth century, more than a century after Newton discovered the various colors within visible light, scientists discovered that there are many types of light that we cannot see with the naked eye.

In 1800, Sir William Herschel discovered **infrared light**. Herschel set out to measure the temperature of various colors of light. He used sunlight and a glass prism to create a spectrum of light. He then placed thermometers under each color of light and compared them to a control thermometer. Herschel noticed that the individual colors of light measured higher than the control thermometer and that the temperature increased from the violet to the red end of the spectrum. He then measured the region just beyond the visible red light and found that the temperature here was the highest of all.

Additional experiments showed that this portion of the light spectrum reflected, refracted, absorbed, and transmitted just like visible light did. Today, we use infrared light in police and military surveillance applications, among other uses, as well as to look through interstellar and intergalactic dust to study star formation and the centers of galaxies.

The following year, the scientist Johann Wilhelm Ritter began experiments to find whether invisible light existed on the other end of the spectrum. Ritter used sunlight and a glass prism to create a spectrum. Then, Ritter placed silver chloride, a substance that darkens when exposed to sunlight, in varying colors of the light spectrum. He showed that the silver chloride darkened more on the violet end of the spectrum than on the red end of the spectrum, which was a known phenomenon. Then he placed silver chloride in the area just beyond the violet end of the spectrum and found that the reaction was even stronger. Ritter had discovered **ultraviolet light**, a type of radiation that we use today for various purposes, from sterilizing medical equipment (and to sanitize pedicure equipment) to studying the composition of stars.

In the late 1880s, the physicist Heinrich Hertz proved the existence of radio waves, which had been theorized by James Maxwell Clerk. Today, we know that visible light, ultraviolet light, infrared light, and radio waves are all part of a larger spectrum called the electromagnetic spectrum.

The electromagnetic spectrum is the range of all types of electromagnetic radiation (energy) from radio waves to visible light to gamma rays and everything in between. We can think of electromagnetic radiation as a stream of massless particles called **photons** that travel in a wave-like pattern at the speed of light. Each photon contains a different amount of energy. Radio waves are made up of the lowest energy photons while gamma rays are made up of the most energetic photons.

Electromagnetic radiation has energy, wavelength, and frequency. The frequency is the number of cycles per second, or hertz (Hz). The wavelength is the length in meters between two wave peaks. The energy is measured in terms of electron volts (eV). For the purpose of studying the universe and its history, wavelength is the most commonly used measurement. Higher energy regions of the spectrum, such as ultraviolet light, X-rays, and gamma rays, have very small wavelengths. Lower energy regions of the spectrum, such as radio waves, have much longer wavelengths.

Spectroscopy

Every object produces a spectrum that varies in the intensity of its radiation at different wavelengths compared to the spectra of other objects. The type of spectra an object emits depends on both its temperature and its chemical composition.

So far, we have discussed continuous spectra of light, or spectra with a full rainbow of color. There are two other important kinds of spectra that help scientists study stars and galaxies: absorption spectra and emission spectra.

The German physicist Gustav Kirchhoff worked closely with the chemist Robert Bunsen to found the field of spectrum analysis. In the 1850s, the two scientists showed that each element gives off a different color light when heated to **incandescence** (the point at which an object emits visible light).

When this light is passed through a prism and split into a light spectrum, each element's resulting spectrum contains a unique pattern of individual wavelengths. Using spectrum analysis, Kirchhoff was able to study the composition of the sun and determine that it contains iron, calcium, magnesium, sodium, nickel, and chromium. (In 1868, Joseph Norman Lockyer used the same technique to determine that the sun contained an unknown element that he named helium after the Greek name for the sun, *helios*.)

Kirchhoff also discovered that when light passes through a gas, the gas absorbs the same wavelengths of light that it would emit if heated.

Kirchhoff created three laws of spectroscopy that describe absorption and emission spectra:

1. A luminous solid, liquid, or dense gas emits light of all wavelengths.
2. A low density, hot gas viewed against a cooler background emits a bright line or emission line spectrum.

3. A low density, cool gas in front of a hotter source of a continuous spectrum creates a dark line or absorption line spectrum.

When we study a star such as our sun, for example, we study its absorption spectra. The star is a hot source of a continuous spectrum and has a cooler atmosphere of gas that absorbs some of that light. When we study incandescent elements in a lab, we see emission spectra.

Though the structure of the atom was not known at the time Kirchhoff made his laws, we know today that the lines in emission and absorption line spectra are created by electrons absorbing or emitting a specific photon.

An individual atom has a positively charged nucleus with one or more negatively charged electrons in orbit around the nucleus. The orbits represent different potential energies—smaller orbits represent smaller amounts of energy. Electrons can jump between energy levels, always instantaneously, when they gain or lose exactly the right amount of energy to make that leap.

An absorption line is created when an atom is excited (such as by absorbing a photon) and jumps from one energy state to another. For example, if a photon with a specific wavelength (121 nanometers, for example) excites a hydrogen atom in its ground state, that photon will be absorbed. Thus, if we look at a source of continuous radiation through a cloud of hydrogen gas, there will be an absorption line at 121 nm.

When an excited atom returns to its ground state, it will emit a photon of the same amount of energy it once absorbed. In this case, the resulting spectrum shows emission lines that precisely correspond to the element's absorption lines.

Redshift

Emission and absorption spectra are very useful for understanding the chemical composition of various stars and galaxies. When it comes to measuring the age of the universe, however, it's even more important to study how the spectral lines of a celestial object have shifted.

When measured in a spectrum, wavelengths of light can shift toward one end of the spectrum or another depending on whether an object is moving toward or away from us. To imagine this phenomenon, consider an ambulance moving toward you. As it first moves closer and then passes you and moves away, its siren seems to change pitch. The siren itself is not changing, however, but the sound wavelengths are compressing and then stretching as it approaches and moves away.

Light waves experience a similar phenomenon. When a celestial object is moving away from Earth, its light wavelengths stretch and elongate, causing the light to appear redder, or **redshifted**. When a celestial object is moving toward Earth (a relatively rare path), its light wavelengths compress and shorten, causing the light to appear bluer, or **blueshifted**.

In 1868, William Huggins noticed that the hydrogen spectrum of the star Sirius was slightly shifted. He interpreted this as the effect of Sirius's radial velocity (movement away) from Earth. Over the next few decades, astronomers began studying the spectra of other stars to determine their radial velocities.

Photons

At the turn of the twentieth century, while studying blackbodies (idealized objects that absorb all incoming radiation) the German physicist Max Planck hypothesized that

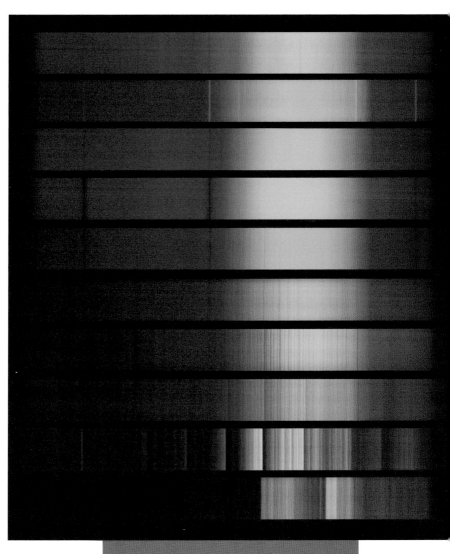

The very red La Superba (bottom spectrum) contains a large proportion of carbon, and the carbon molecules absorb green, blue, and violet light.

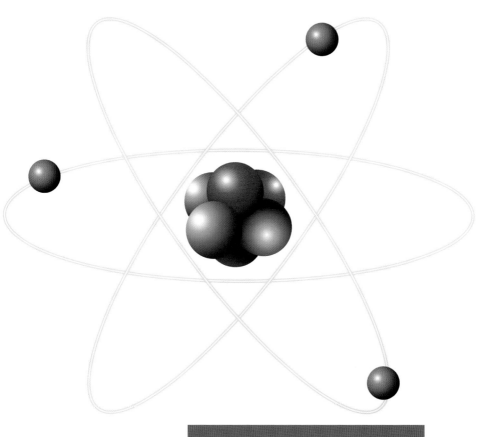

The Bohr model of the atom shows electrons orbiting the nucleus much like the planets orbit the sun.

electromagnetic radiation occurs in discrete bundles of energy called photons.

While much of this book discusses electromagnetic radiation as something that has a wavelength, modern theory holds that light and other particles have characteristics of both waves and particles. As Albert Einstein put it, "We have two contradictory pictures of reality; separately neither of them fully explains the phenomena of light, but together they do." This phenomenon is called the **wave-particle duality**.

Knowing that light behaves as a wave but has **quanta** (discrete amounts) of energy like a particle is especially useful when considering how electromagnetic radiation excites electrons and creates the emission and absorption spectra we learned about in the previous section.

The ATOM

Cosmology and the history of the universe clearly involve the largest known scales of matter and energy, but cosmology also requires an understanding of the very smallest particles as well.

Consider a complex Lego castle set. The Lego box shows an image of the full construction, but to re-create that construction, you must take the individual building blocks and put them together in just the right way. The instructions start with the fundamentals and as you go, the castle looks increasingly like the image on the box.

Reconstructing the history of the universe is something similar, though physicists are still investigating what the very most fundamental building blocks are and how they interact to create the structures and particle interactions we observe today. Particle physics, as this field is called, began with inquiry into the atom.

The atom was first conceived of by the Greek philosopher Demokritos (460 BCE to 370 BCE) as a theoretical unit that makes up all matter and cannot be divided or broken down. In the 1800s, the English chemist John Dalton expanded on this concept and determined that all atoms of a chemical element are identical to one another. In 1897, J. J. Thomson was the first to show that atoms are not the smallest units of matter.

Fourteen years later, in 1911, the Cambridge University physicist Ernest Rutherford discovered the atomic nucleus. Rutherford's graduate student Ernest Marsden conducted an experiment to see what happens when a stream of alpha particles (positively charged particles) was aimed through a piece of gold foil. Detectors around the gold foil measured the path of the particles. Marsden's results showed that a small percentage (about 1 in 20,000) of the particles were scattered at angles greater than 90 degrees. The remainder passed straight through or were deflected at lesser angles.

Rutherford concluded from these results that the positive charge and nearly all of the mass of an atom must be concentrated in a very small region of an atom, which explains why only a small fraction of the particles were strongly deflected. (The positive alpha particles were repelled by the concentrated positive regions of the gold atoms.)

In 1920, Rutherford proposed the name "proton" for the positively charged particles in the nucleus. Rutherford suggested that the nucleus also contains a neutral particle, the neutron, which his one-time graduate student and assistant lab director James Chadwick found in 1932. The neutron became very useful for physicists because as a neutral particle, it could be used to smash and break apart other nuclei. (Neutron bombardment was eventually used to split the uranium atom, which led to the development of the first nuclear bomb.)

For a time, physicists thought that the proton, neutron, and electron were the smallest particles in existence. In 1963, however, Murray Gell-Mann proposed that protons and neutrons are made up of even smaller particles called quarks. Other subatomic particles we know today include neutrinos, positrons, muons, and more.

The SCALE of the UNIVERSE

In the beginning of scientific discourse, academics thought that Earth was at the center of the universe. In a paradigm-shifting development that kicked off the Scientific Revolution, scientists eventually accepted that Earth orbits the sun along with other planets in our solar system. Scientists later discovered that we are part of a galaxy called the Milky Way and the sun is actually

Henrietta Swan Leavitt

The relationship between a Cepheid variable star's **period** and its **luminosity** was discovered by the American astronomer Henrietta Swan Leavitt.

Leavitt was born in 1868 in Lancaster, Massachusetts. She attended Oberlin College before transferring and graduating from the Society for the Collegiate Instruction of Women (today Radcliffe College) in 1892. Leavitt began studying astronomy as a senior in college and continued her studies after graduating from college. Unfortunately, she soon suffered a serious illness that left her severely deaf.

Her hearing loss did not get in the way of her love of astronomy, however. Leavitt volunteered as an assistant at the Harvard Observatory in 1895 and in 1902 became a permanent staff member. She quickly rose to become the head of the photographic stellar photometry department.

Leavitt worked on the observatory's major initiative to determine the brightness of all observable stars. In the course of her work, she invented new methodologies and a standard of photographic measurements that became known as the Harvard Standard. She also discovered more than 2,400 variable stars (about half of the variable stars known at the time).

Most significantly, Leavitt discovered the direct correlation between the length of a Cepheid variable star's period and the star's luminosity. Her discovery would be an instrumental part of paradigm-shifting discoveries by astronomers of the time, including Edwin Hubble.

located quite far from the center. Still, for many years scientists believed that the Milky Way was the only galaxy there was.

In 1924, a young American astronomer named Edwin Hubble shattered the notion that our galaxy was the only galaxy that existed.

Hubble worked at the Mount Wilson Observatory near Pasadena, California, which had the largest telescope of its time, the Hooker Telescope. He trained the telescope on what was then called the Andromeda Nebula, one of the faint clouds of light that were thought to be nebulae within our own galaxy. (Nebulae, or clouds of gas and dust, do exist throughout the universe, but initially galaxies were mistaken for nebulae within the Milky Way.)

Within the Andromeda Nebula Hubble found numerous stars, including a type of star called a Cepheid variable. Cepheid variable stars pulsate at a rate that directly corresponds to their luminosity (intrinsic brightness). After calculating the luminosity based on how often it pulsates (its period), an astronomer can then determine how far away a Cepheid variable star is. (This type of calculation is much like the mental calculation we perform when we see headlights approaching us at night. We know how bright headlights typically are, and if they look very dim, we know that the car must be far away.)

When Hubble calculated how far away the Andromeda Nebula must be based on the period of the Cepheid variable star, he determined that the Andromeda Nebula was not a star cluster within the Milky Way but a galaxy of its own. Today, we know this "nebula" as the Andromeda galaxy, the nearest major galaxy to the Milky Way.

A NEW GRAVITY

One of the most astounding developments in physics of the twentieth century was Albert Einstein's general theory of relativity. Published in 1915, the theory presented a geometric theory of gravity that revised the common understanding of gravity based on Isaac Newton's work centuries earlier.

Newton's theory of gravity held that gravity is a tugging force between two objects that directly depends on the mass of each object and how far away those two objects are from one another. The moon and Earth both attract one another, for example, but the more massive Earth exerts a relatively stronger attractive force on the moon.

In 1905, Einstein had published his special theory of relativity, which in part stated that space and time are inextricably connected in a four-dimensional continuum called space-time. In his 1915 general theory of relativity, Einstein hypothesized that a massive object will create a distortion in space-time much like a bowling ball distorts the surface of a trampoline.

Just like a marble placed on the trampoline will roll inward toward the bowling ball, objects in space follow the distortions in space-time toward more massive objects. In broader terms, matter tells space-time how to curve, and curved space-time tells matter how to move. Light, too, Einstein predicted, would follow any warps in space-time.

On May 29, 1919, a solar eclipse proved Einstein's theory of gravity was more accurate than Newton's. During this particular eclipse, astronomers knew the sun would be passing through the Hyades star cluster. The light from the stars would have to pass through the sun's gravitational field en route to Earth, and because of the darkness from the eclipse, scientists could observe and measure this light when it arrived.

The English physicist and astronomer Sir Arthur Eddington, leader of the experiment, first measured the true positions of the stars in January and February of 1919. When the solar eclipse happened, he measured the star positions again. The star positions appeared shifted due to the path-altering effect, known as gravitational lensing, of the sun's gravitational field.

"LIGHT ALL ASKEW IN THE HEAVENS," the *New York Times* headline read when the results were announced, accompanied by the following subheading: "Men of Science More or Less Agog Over Results of Eclipse Observations."

Einstein's theory of general relativity didn't just change the way we view gravity. It also created enormous new cosmological questions. Depending on how the equations in his theory were solved, the universe was either expanding or contracting. Einstein preferred to believe it was staying static, so he added a term he called the "cosmological constant" to his equations to force it into stability. He would later come to regret this modification of his otherwise elegant equations.

AN EXPANDING UNIVERSE

The final major scientific discovery that laid the foundation for a history of the universe came in 1929 from Edwin Hubble, again using the Hooker Telescope at the Mount Wilson Observatory.

It was by now known that the universe consisted of numerous galaxies. Many, however, believed that the universe was infinite in time and space. To the contrary, Hubble and his assistant Milton Humason published a paper showing that galaxies were moving away from Earth and that the farther away a galaxy was, the faster it was moving away.

Hubble had again used Cepheid variable stars and other ways of determining distance to plot the distance of each galaxy from Earth. He studied the redshift of each galaxy to plot each galaxy's radial velocity. The resulting graph was very clear: galaxies are moving away from Earth at a speed directly correlated to their distance from us.

Hubble's work shattered the notion that the universe existed in some kind of stasis or that it had remained the same size for infinity. It also raised a curious question: If all of the galaxies were moving away from our own galaxy, where had those galaxies been relative to one another in the past?

The answer to that question was the foundation of the big bang theory, the modern standard cosmological model.

The horrors of World War I deeply impacted Georges Lemaître and shifted his career path from engineering to priesthood and theoretical physics.

CHAPTER 3

The Major Players in the Big Bang Theory

S ome discoveries, like Alexander Fleming's 1928 discovery of penicillin, come from a single scientist. Others, like the big bang theory, are created by many scientists over time.

The big bang theory took enormous amounts of foundational science, as shown in the previous chapter, followed by theoretical proposals and tangible discoveries that helped create a narrative of the first few seconds of our universe and the billions of years that followed.

EARLY TWENTIETH CENTURY

The first murmurs of an expanding universe, including a model that began with a big bang, came in the early twentieth century.

Albert Einstein's theory of general relativity raised an enormous question of the future of the universe. Was it expanding, was it contracting, or was it staying the same? In 1927, Georges Lemaître proposed a theory of an expanding universe, but it was largely ignored at first. Two years later, Edwin Hubble's groundbreaking work at Mount Wilson Observatory provided a clear answer: the universe was expanding over time.

In the 1920s, Einstein's focus turned to finding a unified field theory that would bring all forces of the universe into one framework.

Albert Einstein

Albert Einstein was born in 1879 in Ulm, Germany, a city whose motto was "Ulmenses sunt mathematici" or "the people of Ulm are mathematicians." His family moved to Munich when he was six weeks old.

Albert's speech was slow to develop, but contrary to popular belief, he was an excellent student. He was also a rebellious student, however, and questioned authority and the teaching methods at his academy.

As a child, Albert became fascinated with science when he was home sick from school and his father brought him a compass. Albert was intrigued by the power of a hidden force field on the compass's needle, later writing, "I can still remember—or at least I believe I can remember—that this experience made a deep and lasting impression on me … Something deeply hidden had to be behind things."

Albert attended a high school, the Luitpold Gymnasium, that emphasized math and science. He got top marks in his courses and was far ahead of the school's standards in math. In his adolescence, he devoured books on math and science and developed a strong aversion to religion. Yet his deep suspicion of authority created trouble for him at school.

When the family business went under, his family moved to northern Italy and left fifteen-year-old Albert behind to finish his studies in Munich. Albert left the school that Christmas, however, and joined his family in Italy, vowing to never go back to Germany. He later finished school in Aurau, Switzerland, before entering the Zurich Polytechnic.

Einstein graduated from university in 1900. He had trouble finding a professorship and ended up accepting a job at the patent office in Bern in 1902. The menial position afforded him both the spare time and the intellectual freedom to develop the ideas that would one day make him famous. In 1905, he made his first foray into fame. That year, Einstein published five papers that changed physics forever, including one with his famous equation, $E=mc^2$, and another with his special theory of relativity.

Another of these papers, on molecular measurements, finally earned Einstein his PhD. He became a lecturer at the University of Bern in 1908, a junior professor at the University of Zurich in 1909, a professor of theoretical physics in Prague in 1911, and a professor at the University of Berlin in 1914.

When Einstein published his general theory of relativity in 1915, Hubble had not yet discovered galaxies beyond the Milky Way. Most astronomers at this time, including Einstein, believed that the universe consisted of just our Milky Way and its approximately one hundred billion stars. Most, again including Einstein, also believed that the universe was in an overall stable state, neither expanding nor shrinking.

Edwin Hubble's discoveries of the Andromeda galaxy and the direct correlation between the distance of a galaxy from Earth and its recession speed shook Einstein's understanding of the universe. He dismissed his cosmological constant and embraced the expanding universe, and on his second visit to America, Einstein took a trip to Mount Wilson to pay a call on Hubble and the Hooker Telescope.

Einstein was in California when Adolf Hitler took power in 1933, and Einstein never went back to Germany. He stayed in America, where he became a professor of theoretical physics at the Institute for Advanced Study in Princeton, New Jersey. He held this post until his retirement in 1945. In addition to his contribution to physics, Einstein wrote significantly on pacifism, helped dozens of Jewish refugees enter the United States, and supported the foundation of a Jewish state. He was offered the presidency of Israel in 1952, but he declined.

Einstein enjoyed playing the violin, which helped him work through difficult problems, as well as sailing. During his life, he won numerous prizes including the 1921 Nobel Prize. He died in 1955.

The Hooker Telescope has received control systems and optics upgrades over the years and is still used today.

Edwin Hubble

Edwin Hubble was born in Missouri in 1889 and moved to Chicago with his family at the age of nine. He attended the University of Chicago, where he obtained a degree in mathematics and astronomy in 1910. He earned a Rhodes scholarship to study at Oxford University, where he switched his studies to law to keep a promise to his father. After three years, he obtained a law degree and returned to the United States.

In 1914 Hubble switched back to astronomy, enrolling in a PhD program at Chicago University. "I knew that even if I were second or third rate, it was astronomy that mattered," he said. He was offered a job at the Mount Wilson Observatory in 1917, but he postponed his acceptance to enlist in the military. After serving briefly in France, Hubble returned to the United States and began his post at the Mount Wilson Observatory in 1919.

Hubble worked for decades at the observatory. He served again in World War II as a supervisor at the Aberdeen Proving Ground in Maryland (a location for ordnance design and testing), for which he earned a Medal of Merit in 1946. He also helped design and construct the Hale Telescope, a 200-inch (5-meter) telescope on Palomar Mountain. Hubble died in 1953.

Georges Lemaître

Georges Lemaître was born in Charleroi, Belgium, in 1894. Lemaître initially studied engineering before volunteering for the Belgian army and serving as an artillery officer during World War I. During the war, Lemaître witnessed the first poison gas attack in history and was decorated with the Croix de Guerre (Cross of War).

Post-war, Lemaître switched his scientific focus from engineering to mathematics and physics. He obtained a doctorate from the University of Louvain in 1920 and was ordained as a priest in 1923. Lemaître received a traveling scholarship from the Belgian government, awarded for a thesis he wrote on relativity and gravitation, that allowed him to spend the subsequent years studying at Cambridge University, the Harvard College Observatory, and the Massachusetts Institute of Technology. He returned to the University of Louvain in 1925 and became a full professor of astrophysics there in 1927.

That same year, Lemaître proposed that the universe had begun at a finite moment in a highly condensed state and had expanded ever since. He published his theory in the *Annals of the Scientific Society of Brussels*, which was not widely read outside of Belgium. Some who did read it dismissed his work as influenced by his theological studies, as the idea of a beginning could imply a divine creator. Lemaître disliked religious readings of his cosmology, however, arguing that his theory "remains entirely outside any metaphysical or religious question."

Everything changed for Lemaître when his former Cambridge University professor Sir Arthur Eddington began to champion Lemaître's work. Eddington, who had observed the 1919 eclipse, had seen the initial publication but forgot about it for some time. In 1930, three years after Lemaître first published his expansion theory and one year after Hubble released his data on the expanding universe, Eddington wrote a letter to the journal *Nature* drawing attention to Lemaître's work. In hindsight, with Hubble's data as evidence, Lemaître's work was significantly easier to accept.

Einstein had read Lemaître's 1927 paper and originally told him that his math was correct but his physics were abominable. After Hubble's data was published, however, Einstein was much more interested in what Lemaître had to say about cosmology, and the two had many walks and talks together over the following years.

After publishing on his primeval atom theory, Lemaître's academic work included cosmic rays, celestial mechanics, and pioneering work on using computers to solve astrophysical problems. He received numerous awards, including the Royal Astronomical Society's first Eddington Medal in 1953. Lemaître died in 1966.

MID-TWENTIETH CENTURY

Einstein, Hubble, and Lemaître laid the foundation for modern cosmology. Einstein's general theory of relativity raised curious questions about the universe, Lemaître published a theory of a universe with a finite beginning and original highly condensed state, and Hubble's data provided evidence that the universe was indeed expanding over time.

Over the subsequent decades, numerous scientists would propose theories that built on that foundation and make discoveries that helped create the standard big bang model of cosmology. George Gamow and Ralph Alpher proposed a modification of Lemaître's work in which all of the elements were formed in the big bang. Fred Hoyle opposed the big bang model, but his work on **stellar nucleosynthesis** helped fill in scientific gaps in the theory. Arno Penzias and Robert Wilson unintentionally discovered strong evidence of the big bang, and George Smoot designed a massive experiment to find whether that evidence could also explain the formation of stars and galaxies over time.

George Gamow

George Gamow was born in Odessa, Ukraine (it was part of the Russian Empire at the time), in 1904. He loved science from a young age, growing interested in astronomy when his father gave him a telescope for his thirteenth birthday.

Gamow graduated from the University of Leningrad in 1928 and moved to Göttingen, Germany, where he developed a theory of radioactive decay as a function of **quantum mechanics**. He was the first to successfully explain why some

Alexander Friedmann

Like Lemaître, Alexander Friedmann also solved Einstein's equations of general relativity and proposed an expanding model of the universe in the 1920s. Friedmann and his theory received significantly less attention than Lemaître, however, due to Friedmann's background as a mathematician (not a physicist) and his death in 1925, before Hubble had shown that the universe was indeed expanding.

Friedmann was born in 1888 in St. Petersburg, Russia. As a student, Friedmann showed a remarkable talent for mathematics and coauthored a paper published in *Mathematicshe Annalen* in 1905. During World War I, Friedmann joined the volunteer aviation detachment and flew in bombing raids.

After the war, Friedmann worked in various positions including as head of the Central Aeronautical Station in Kiev, as a professor at the University of Perm, and as director of the Main Geophysical Observatory in Leningrad. The cosmologist George Gamow briefly studied under Friedmann at the observatory.

Friedmann became interested in Einstein's general theory of relativity and published an article, "On the Curvature of Space," in 1922 that proposed a dynamic, expanding universe. Einstein quickly rejected Friedmann's work in the same journal, *Zeitschrift für Physik*, though he retracted his rejection again in the journal in 1923.

Friedmann's equations for the expansion of space, known as the Friedmann equations, show the fate of the universe as either expanding forever, expanding forever at a decreasing rate, or collapsing backward (dependent on its density).

Friedmann's career in cosmology was cut short in 1925 when he died of typhus.

Gamow became a professor at the University of Colorado at Boulder in 1956 and worked there until his death.

radioactive elements decay in seconds while others slowly decay over millennia.

The theoretical physicist Niels Bohr offered Gamow a fellowship at the Theoretical Physics Institute of the University of Copenhagen where, among other work, Gamow worked on calculations of stellar thermonuclear reactions. Gamow also convinced the experimental physicist Ernest Rutherford of the value in building a proton accelerator, which was later used to split a lithium nucleus into alpha particles.

As much of Europe faced the pressures of communism and fascism in the 1930s, many intellectuals fled the continent (including Einstein). Gamow made several attempts to escape the Soviet Union, including an attempted crossing of the Black Sea into Turkey via kayak in 1932. He finally got his chance to escape when he was invited to give a talk in Brussels on the properties of the atomic nuclei. Gamow arranged for his wife, Rho, also a physicist, to accompany him. From there, the Gamows traveled through Europe and then to America in pursuit of an academic career outside of the Soviet Union.

Though he hoped for a prestigious position at a school known for its physics program, Gamow ended up accepting a position at George Washington University, which at the time didn't have a strong reputation in physics. Gamow quickly changed that, however, as his terms of acceptance involved expanding the physics department at GWU and establishing a theoretical physics conference series.

In addition to developing a theory of element formation in the big bang, Gamow's research included stellar evolution, supernovas, and red giants. In later years, Gamow made contributions in biochemistry as well as a foray into what he called "the physics of living matter." After reading about Watson and Crick's work on the structure of DNA in the journal *Nature*, he wrote his own note to *Nature* proposing the existence of a genetic code within DNA that was determined by the "composition of its unique complement of proteins" made up of chains of amino acids. Gamow's ideas inspired Watson, Crick, and many other researchers to begin researching how DNA coded proteins.

Gamow also wrote numerous popular books designed to give non-physicists access to complex topics, including the Mr. Tomkins series about a toy universe with properties different from our own and *One, Two, Three…Infinity*. Gamow died in 1968.

Ralph Alpher

Ralph Alpher was born in 1921 in Washington, DC, to immigrant parents. He was accepted into the Massachusetts Institute of Technology but his scholarship was withdrawn after he met with an alumnus. Alpher always suspected the sudden change happened because he had told the alumnus of his Jewish heritage. Instead, Alpher enrolled at George Washington University, where he obtained his undergraduate, master's, and doctoral degrees.

Alpher began his contributions to cosmology when he worked on the synthesis of elements in the big bang with his dissertation advisor George Gamow. The paper was published on April 1, 1948. As an April Fool's joke, Gamow listed physicist Hans Bethe as a coauthor "in absentia" so that the byline would read "Alpher-Bethe-Gamow," a play on the first three letters of the Greek alphabet. As a result of Gamow's joke, Alpher's contributions to the research were overlooked as many assumed the more senior Bethe had played a more significant role than young Alpher.

Alpher continued his work on nucleosynthesis with another physicist, Robert Herman, publishing numerous papers on nucleosynthesis and the early universe. They predicted that the radiation left over from the early universe should be about 5 degrees K in the present universe and encouraged scientists to look for this radiation.

The reception toward Alpher and Herman's work was cool, and both left academia. Alpher accepted a job at General Electric, where he worked in research and development for thirty-two years.

Later in life, Alpher's predictions were proven true when Arno Penzias and Robert Wilson found the relic radiation from the big bang at a temperature in accordance with Alpher and Herman's predictions. Still, Alpher's contributions to the big bang model of cosmology were largely overlooked in favor of Penzias, Wilson, and Gamow until recent decades. The continued slights and lack of inclusion in big bang science accolades haunted him. Alpher died in 2007.

Fred Hoyle

Sir Fred Hoyle was one of the biggest opponents of the big bang theory but also the man who gave it its name and a contributor to its development.

Hoyle was born in Yorkshire, England, in 1915. He attended Emmanuel College and Cambridge University and worked on radar development for six years during World War II. He then returned to Cambridge, where he lectured in mathematics.

In 1948, Hoyle, the astronomer Thomas Gold, and the mathematician Hermann Bondi developed the **steady state** theory, which holds that the universe is expanding but that new matter is continuously being created such that the mean density of matter in space remains a constant. As galaxies move away, new galaxies emerge between them, such that the large-scale properties of the universe remain the same over time.

Hoyle's work included more than a decade of research that demonstrated that all of the elements from carbon and up to iron could be synthesized inside of stars as a result of nuclear fusion. In 1957, Hoyle, along with Margaret Burbidge, Geoffrey Burbidge, and William Fowler, published a paper showing that even heavier elements could be produced by stars through supernovas.

Hoyle also appeared in a series of radio talks on astronomy in the 1940s, in which he used the term "big bang" to mock his rival physicists. The term stuck, just as the big bang theory itself did.

Hoyle also wrote on the possibility that life originated in space, as well as many science fiction books such as *The Molecule Men* and the *Monster of Loch Ness*; a television series, *A for Andromeda*; and a play, *Rockets in Ursa Major*. Hoyle was knighted in 1972 and died in 2001.

Arno Penzias

Arno Penzias was born in Munich, Germany, in 1933 to a Jewish family. His family was rounded up for deportation to Poland when he was a young boy, but they returned to Munich after a number of days. His parents, aware of the danger they faced, sent Arno and his younger brother on a train to England in 1939.

His parents were able to join the two boys in England and, after six months there, they moved to New York City. Penzias attended the City College of New York, a municipally funded college dedicated to educating the children of New York's immigrants. After college, he spent two years in the Army Signal Corps, which develops and manages communication and information systems for the command and control of the military.

When he began his graduate studies in physics at Columbia University in 1956, that army experience helped Penzias gain research projects in the Columbia radiation laboratory. For his thesis, he built a maser amplifier, a device that amplifies electromagnetic radiation, for a radio astronomy experiment.

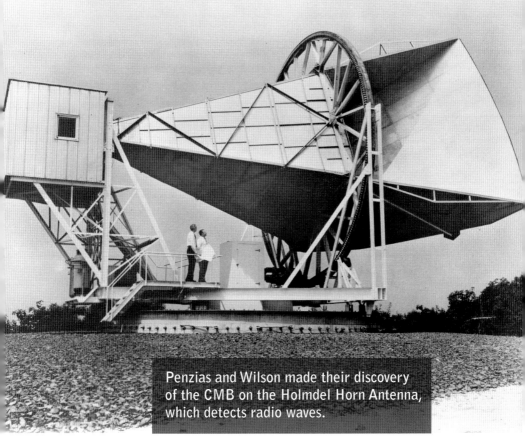

Penzias and Wilson made their discovery of the CMB on the Holmdel Horn Antenna, which detects radio waves.

After finishing his PhD, Penzias began working at Bell Labs in Holmdel, New Jersey. There, Penzias was able to continue his work in radio astronomy, which led to his work with fellow radio astronomer Robert Wilson. In an attempt to measure the radiation intensity of the Milky Way, the two accidentally discovered the cosmic microwave background (CMB) radiation, the relic radiation left over from the big bang.

Penzias rose through numerous levels of leadership at Bell Labs, eventually becoming vice president of research. As his own astrophysics research wound down, he wrote a book called *Ideas and Information* on the creation and use of technology in society. When he approached a mandatory retirement age, Penzias left the research and development world for Silicon Valley, where he became involved in the venture capital world.

Robert Wilson

Robert Wilson was born in Houston, Texas, in 1936. His father worked for an oil well service company, and while in high school Robert often accompanied his father into the oil fields. His parents were both "inveterate do-it-yourselfers," Wilson wrote, and he gained a particular fondness for electronics from his father. As a high school student, Robert enjoyed repairing radios and television sets.

Wilson attended Rice University, where he majored in physics. He obtained his PhD in physics at Caltech, where he worked with radio astronomer John Bolton on expanding a radio map of the Milky Way. After graduation, he joined Bell Labs' radio research department. Together, Wilson and Penzias made numerous discoveries using radio astronomy, including a surprising abundance of carbon monoxide in the Milky Way and their Nobel Prize–winning discovery of the CMB.

Today, Wilson continues to live in Holmdel, NJ, with his family.

George Smoot

George Smoot grew up attending university biology courses with his mother. Both parents had resumed their college educations after World War II and two children, and watching his parents study, learn, and dedicate time to education had a strong influence on George. After some financial difficulties, the family moved to Alaska, where George spent his time outside exploring and studying the night sky.

George's father worked for the United States Geological Survey, and as his reputation as a field scientist grew, he traveled around the world to gather data on the properties and water flow of rivers. George's parents played a shaping role in his life through high school, as his father tutored him in trigonometry and calculus while his mother gave him lessons in science and history.

Smoot attended the Massachusetts Institute of Technology (MIT), where he majored in mathematics and physics. He stayed at MIT for his PhD and then moved to Berkeley to work on particle physics at the Lawrence Berkeley National Laboratory. There, he worked on the High-Altitude Particle Physics Experiment, in which Smoot and his colleagues searched for evidence of the big bang using balloon-borne detectors that would look for antimatter in cosmic rays.

Smoot eventually changed his focus to studying the CMB for more information about the early universe, which led to his Nobel Prize–winning discovery of fluctuations in the CMB.

Putting It Together

Over the twentieth century, the big bang theory slowly fell into place. In the next chapter, we'll discuss the initial versions of the theory and the current big bang model of cosmology.

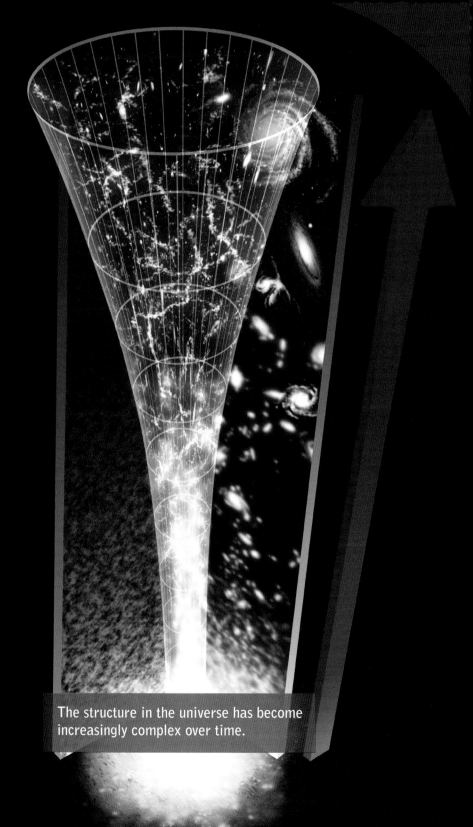

The structure in the universe has become increasingly complex over time.

CHAPTER 4

The Discovery of the Big Bang

As scientists studied the origins of the universe, their cosmological research focused on three major pillars: the expanding universe, nucleosynthesis, and the cosmic microwave background radiation. Today, all three give strong support for the big bang model while also providing clarity into how the universe evolved over time.

The EXPANDING UNIVERSE

"The whole story of the world need not have been written down in the first quantum like a song on the disc of a phonograph. The whole matter of the world must have been present at the beginning, but the story it has to tell may be written step by step."

—Georges Lemaître

In the 1920s, two academics independently worked through Einstein's general relativity equations and found that the solutions suggested an expanding universe. One was Alexander

Friedmann, whose work in the field was cut short by his untimely death from typhoid fever in 1925. The other was Georges Lemaître, who went on to become the first scientist to propose a theory of an expanding universe with a discrete beginning. Today, Lemaître is known as the father of the big bang theory.

The Primeval Atom

Lemaître was an avid scholar of general relativity and studied under one of its foremost experts, Sir Arthur Eddington, at Cambridge University in England. Lemaître began writing about an expanding universe in the 1920s. In the early 1930s, he added the concept of a discrete origin to his theory.

In a 1931 letter published in the journal *Nature*, Lemaître began by writing, "Sir Arthur Eddington states that, philosophically, the notion of a beginning of the present order of Nature is repugnant to him …" For many scientists like Eddington any cosmology with a finite beginning had too much of a creation narrative, which harkened back to mythology and supernatural forces, to be scientifically acceptable.

To Lemaître, the notion of a beginning of the universe was not only quite acceptable, it was the logical conclusion from quantum theory. If there was a constant total amount of energy in the universe and that number of distinct quanta were increasing, as theory held, then the implication must be that there were once much fewer quanta, perhaps a single quantum, that held all of the energy in the universe.

In the letter to *Nature*, Lemaître suggested the possibility of a single unique radioactive atom that held all the mass in the universe before decaying into smaller and smaller atoms.

"The last two thousand million years are slow evolution: they are ashes and smoke of bright but very rapid fireworks," he wrote in a paper called "The Evolution of the Universe." In a later text, *The Primeval Atom*, he wrote: "We can compare space-time to an open, conic cup … The bottom of the cup is the origin of atomic disintegration; it is the first instant at the bottom of space-time, the now which has no yesterday because, yesterday, there was no space."

Lemaître was the first physicist to propose a widely discussed model of cosmology with a finite beginning and expansion from a single atom. However, his theory of cosmology wasn't the big bang we think of today, which involves an explosion of pure energy that converts into all of the matter in the known universe. Lemaître's model was a colder, disintegrating model of the universe. The hot big bang model that we know today arrived seventeen years later.

NUCLEOSYNTHESIS

Lemaître worked on his cosmology in the years between World War I and World War II. World War II temporarily interrupted astrophysics as it diverted many top physicists to war projects and isolated others. Lemaître himself was cut off in Belgium after the Germans invaded, and he nearly died in an Allied forces' bombing of his apartment building.

After the war, Lemaître turned his focus to other scientific pursuits, including mathematical computing. Einstein turned his attention to finding a unified field theory that would unite general relativity with quantum mechanics. Sir Arthur Eddington died in 1944. One generation of scientists stepped away from the cosmological question; a new generation of scientists stepped up.

Roughly a decade after Lemaître proposed a primeval atom that decayed into all the matter in the universe, George Gamow

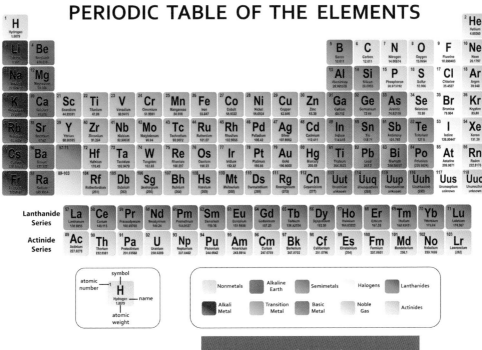

PERIODIC TABLE OF THE ELEMENTS

To be successful, big bang cosmologists had to explain how elements heavier than lithium formed in the universe.

and Ralph Alpher published a paper detailing the foundation of the modern big bang theory.

Gamow's early work included studying radioactivity and stellar physics. When World War II broke out, Gamow had plenty of time to focus on the implications of nuclear physics on cosmology. While other American scientists were drafted to support the war effort, Gamow was left out because he had briefly served in the Red Army before fleeing Ukraine.

Years later, as a professor at George Washington University, Gamow and his doctoral student Ralph Alpher published a paper outlining their theory of the beginning of the universe and synthesis of matter. The physicists Carl von Weizsäcker and Hans Bethe had both showed how stars convert hydrogen into helium through what is called the carbon-nitrogen-oxygen cycle, but at the time no physicist could explain how heavier elements, or even carbon, were formed within stars. Gamow believed they could have formed in the beginning of the universe.

Gamow and Alpher proposed that the universe did not begin as a single super atom but as hot, highly compressed neutron gas that underwent a rapid expansion and cooling. The initial primordial matter decayed into protons and electrons as the gas pressure dropped due to the expansion. (Gas pressure is a function of molecular collisions. As the gas density of the early universe decreased, the particles collided less frequently and the pressure dropped.)

This began a process called **big bang nucleosynthesis** in which protons "captured" neutrons to form deuterium (an isotope of hydrogen). Neutron capture continued and formed heavier and heavier elements by adding one neutron and one proton at a time.

The relative abundance of elements was determined by the time allowed by the universe's expansion (that is, the time in which the universe had the right conditions for nucleosynthesis to proceed). This capped window of time, Gamow and Alpher believed, explained why light hydrogen was so prevalent and heavy elements like gold so rare. Their 1948 paper contained a model for only the abundances of hydrogen and helium, but as these two elements account for 99 percent of the atoms in the universe, it was enough to make their paper credible.

In Alpher's PhD thesis, he wrote that the nucleosynthesis of hydrogen and helium took just three hundred seconds.

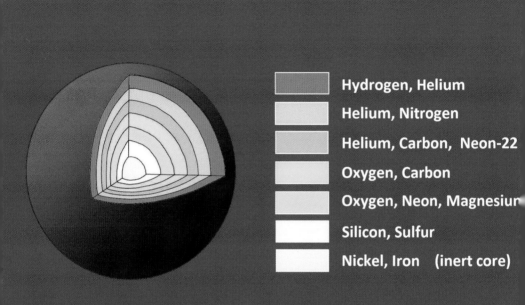

	Hydrogen, Helium
	Helium, Nitrogen
	Helium, Carbon, Neon-22
	Oxygen, Carbon
	Oxygen, Neon, Magnesiur
	Silicon, Sulfur
	Nickel, Iron (inert core)

Over time, large stars fuse successively heavier elements, creating "shells" of different elements that are eventually released into the universe.

Alpher's calculations showed that there should be about ten hydrogen nuclei for every helium nucleus at the end of the big bang, which matches modern observed abundances and lent further support to the model.

In another 1948 paper, Alpher and his coauthor Robert Herman calculated that the radiation from the beginning of the universe should today be about 5 degrees K. This prediction provided a way to test the theory and provide strong supporting evidence for its validity.

Gamow and Alpher's work created a buzz in the scientific community because it explained the origin of the most abundant elements and provided a compelling narrative of the big bang. Their work created the basic model of the big bang theory we know today.

The Synthesis of Heavier Elements

There were problems with Gamow and Alpher's work, however, namely that elements cannot be formed through neutron capture because there is no stable nucleus with five neutrons. Big bang nucleosynthesis cannot proceed past lithium, and the heavier elements must be created through some other process.

In just a few decades, however, this issue was resolved. In 1957, Fred Hoyle and the American physicist Willy Fowler at Caltech showed that hydrogen nuclei could fuse into helium nuclei and subsequently into beryllium, carbon, oxygen, and so on inside of stars. In Gamow and Alpher's big bang nucleosynthesis model, this chain had broken down. In Hoyle and Fowler's stellar nucleosynthesis model, however, it worked—so long as a special state of carbon-12 (the most common isotope of carbon) existed. Fowler was able to create this excited state of carbon-12 in the lab, proving that the chain worked.

Hoyle and Fowler's results showed that the lightest elements could have been created in the big bang and subsequent element formation could have continued inside of stars. With this new, stronger model of nucleosynthesis, the big bang model gained strength.

The Age of the Universe

One other roadblock that had to be cleared before the big bang model was embraced by the scientific community was the age of the universe.

After Hubble's discovery of the expanding universe, astronomers used his measurements to calculate the age of the universe. Galaxies move away from each other at a velocity represented by $v = H_0 \times D$. V is the observed velocity of the galaxy as it moves away from us, D is the distance to the galaxy, and H is the **Hubble constant**. The Hubble constant represents the expansion rate of the universe, and Hubble's 1929 estimate of this value was about 500 kilometers per second per **megaparsec** (Mpc). (Parsecs are measurements of distance in astronomy. One parsec is 3.26 light-years long, and one megaparsec is 3.26 million light-years long.)

The Hubble constant can be used to infer the age of the galaxy. If the universe had been expanding at a rate of 500 km/s/Mpc to present day, the universe was about 1.8 billion years old. However, geologists had shown through examinations of radioactive rocks that Earth was older than 1.8 billion years, and it was assumed that stars were even older than our planet. This timescale difficulty, as it was called, was a major flaw in the big bang models proposed by Lemaître and Gamow.

It turned out, however, that Hubble's measurements weren't entirely accurate. The German astronomer Walter Baade discovered that there were two major types of Cepheid variable stars, which Hubble didn't know when he used Cepheid variables to calculate the distance to the Andromeda galaxy. The younger Population I stars are hotter, brighter, and bluer than the older Population II stars. Hubble had observed Population I Cepheid variable stars in Andromeda but mistook them for dimmer Population II stars. He saw a relatively bright star and, with the dimmer stars in mind, thought it must be much closer than it really was.

Baade recalculated the distance to Andromeda using the knowledge of both types of Cepheid variables. His new calculation showed that Andromeda was twice as far away as previously thought. It also opened up a new look at the big bang model's timeline: if the recession speeds remained the same but the distances doubled, the age of the universe was now around 3.6 billion years. Baade formally announced his results in 1952, just four years after Gamow and Alpher published their first paper on big bang nucleosynthesis.

This was much better for the big bang model as it allowed for a universe that was older than Earth, but it wasn't yet a complete success. There were other elements of the universe thought to be older than 3.6 billion years.

Baade's student Allan Sandage took on the task of measuring the distances to the farthest galaxies. Previously, due to technological limitations, astronomers had to use a variety of assumptions to measure the distance to very far-off galaxies. One of those assumptions rested on finding the brightest star in a faraway galaxy. By comparing its apparent (observed) brightness to the **apparent brightness** of the brightest stars in a closer galaxy, astronomers could come up with a rough estimate of how far away the distant galaxy was. However, Sandage showed that what astronomers thought was the brightest star was actually often an enormous, very luminous cloud of hydrogen gas.

That meant that the actual brightest star in the distant galaxies was much dimmer than was previously known and the galaxies were much farther off then previously calculated. Sandage revised the age of the universe to first 5.5 billion years in 1954 and eventually to an age between 10 billion and 20 billion years.

The new timeline allowed for all of the planets, stars, and galaxies to form and thus made the big bang model compatible with observations of the universe.

Today, the age of the universe is estimated to be 13.8 billion years, within Sandage's later estimated range. (The Hubble constant, H_0, is now estimated to be somewhere between 45 km/sec/Mpc to 90 km/sec/Mpc.) The current age estimate has been calculated using a variety of methods, including measurements of stellar evolution, expansion of the universe, and radioactive decay, with all three methods in agreement of the universe's age.

The COSMIC MICROWAVE BACKGROUND

Alpher and Herman predicted that the universe would contain radiation from the big bang that in modern day would have stretched and cooled to 5 degrees K. At the time, nobody went looking for this testable prediction of the big bang model. Arno Penzias and Robert Wilson discovered the relic radiation entirely by accident in 1965.

Discovering the CMB

The two radio astronomers were using the Holmdel Horn Antenna in Holmdel, New Jersey, to map the radio waves coming from the Milky Way. When they began their data collection, they found that there was a persistent radio signal that came from every direction at all times of day and night. It hissed like static on a radio. And like static on the radio, it was annoying.

The noise that Penzias and Wilson picked up was not actually so significant as to prohibit them from making their desired measurements. In fact, it was weak enough that other astronomers had dismissed the noise and therefore missed its significance. Penzias and Wilson were not so easily put off, however. For months, the two astronomers tried everything they could think of to remove or reduce this interfering "noise."

They tried pointing the antenna toward New York City to see if the cause was some sort of city-related interference. They took the antenna apart, looked for defects, and put it back together. The swept out droppings from a pair of pigeons nesting inside the antenna and, eventually, trapped the pigeons and got rid of them.

None of these efforts helped. It seemed that the sky itself was glowing with faint radio light in all directions at a temperature of 3 degrees K.

Penzias and Wilson learned through another scientist that a Princeton University physicist, Robert Dicke, had predicted (like Alpher and Herman) that the big bang would have left residual radiation. Dicke was about to design an experiment looking for the radiation left over from the big bang when Penzias called him up to discuss what he and Wilson had found.

In the early universe, when conditions were still too hot for electrons to bond with atomic nuclei, photons of light scattered off the free electrons much like rays of light scatter off drops of water in the fog. When the hot universe cooled enough for the free electrons to bond with the nuclei to form neutral atoms in a moment called **recombination**, the light that filled the universe was suddenly able to move freely.

When the light first broke free from the fog of electrons, a process called **photon decoupling**, it had a wavelength of about one-thousandth of a millimeter. Over the course of billions of years and into the twentieth century, its wavelength stretched to about a millimeter in length. At this wavelength, the radiation was now in the radio portion of the electromagnetic spectrum. More specifically, the wavelength belongs to the microwave subsection of the radio spectrum, giving it the name "cosmic microwave background," or CMB.

Penzias and Wilson had discovered the relic radiation that Alpher and Herman had predicted decades before and that Dicke had predicted more recently in the 1960s.

(You might have seen the CMB for yourself on an old television. On a fuzzy screen between channels, 1 percent of the static on the screen is the microwave radiation left over from the big bang.)

This discovery was the first tested prediction of the big bang model of cosmology and the most convincing evidence that the model was accurate. Penzias and Wilson's discovery finally turned the big bang model of cosmology into a mainstream scientific theory.

However, another question remained. If the big bang model was correct, how did galaxies and stars form in the young universe? In general, the cosmic microwave background was a smooth glow across the whole universe. It was thought that the big bang explosion had created an even expanse of matter. How could structure form from such a smooth cosmic soup?

Mapping the CMB

Those who supported the big bang model believed that the early universe must not have been perfectly uniform, for otherwise stars and galaxies *couldn't* have formed. Instead, they imagined a universe where some areas were denser than others, creating regions where gravity would eventually attract more matter and cause the regions to collapse under their own weight.

There was no proof of these variations in density when Penzias and Wilson first discovered the CMB. The signal they picked up was uniform across time and space. The American astronomer George Smoot hoped that if he measured the CMB with more powerful instruments, he would find the predicted density variations.

Smoot worked at the University of California at Berkeley, where he participated in several 1970s experiments using giant balloons to lift radiation detectors tens of kilometers above Earth. The scientists hoped that this high altitude would remove any radiation from microwaves in Earth's atmosphere. However, the cold temperatures at that altitude could wreak havoc on the detectors and the balloons were prone to crash-landing.

In efforts to find other means of studying the CMB from high altitudes, Smoot used a United States Air Force spy plane to take a detector up. The data gathered ended up showing that the Milky Way was moving through the universe at a speed of 600,000 kilometers per second, which was new and interesting information, but not the data Smoot intended to find.

While his 1976 spy plane experiment was underway, Smoot began working on designing a satellite detector called COBE, or the Cosmic Background Explorer. COBE contained several detectors including a Differential Microwave Radiometer (DMR) that measured the CMB radiation from two separate directions and found the difference. The DMR could thus detect whether the CMB was perfectly smooth or had small fluctuations.

COBE was scheduled to launch in 1988, but the experiment ran into a problem when the *Challenger* space shuttle exploded in January of 1986. NASA upended its flight schedule and called off the scheduled COBE launch.

The COBE team explored opportunities to launch on a foreign rocket, namely with the French, but NASA objected. Eventually, NASA agreed to send COBE up in a Delta rocket, which was much smaller than they had initially planned for. The team quickly redesigned COBE to be smaller and lighter so the sophisticated equipment could fit in the rocket.

COBE launched on November 18, 1989. It took about six months to complete an initial rough, full-sky survey. The initial data showed no variations, but when the first thorough full-sky map was complete in December of 1991, the data showed something more. The peak wavelength of the CMB radiation varied by 0.001 percent, a tiny variation but significant enough to show that the early universe was inhomogeneous. The variations were big enough to cause matter to clump and, eventually, galaxies to form.

Smoot's team announced their results in April of 1992. It was one of the most significant discoveries in the history of cosmology, for the COBE results showed that the big bang model of cosmology could explain the history of the universe from its birth to the formation of galaxies to present day. Subsequent missions by the WMAP and Planck satellites confirmed and refined COBE's measurements of the CMB.

By the 1990s, all three pillars of the big bang model were in place and the big bang became the standard cosmological model for our universe.

Over the past few decades, scientists have arrived at a sophisticated, detailed standard model of those first few moments in the infant universe.

The STANDARD MODEL

In the first half of this chapter, we looked at how the discovery of the big bang fell into place, piece by piece. Now, let's dig in deeper to the details of how it worked.

The standard model of the big bang today contains details of the first fractions of a second. The numbers at this time in the universe's history are both astronomically small and astronomically large. As a quick refresher on scientific notation, 10^{-43} seconds is the equivalent of a decimal place followed by 42 zeroes and a one, or 0.00000000000000000000 00000000000000000001 seconds.

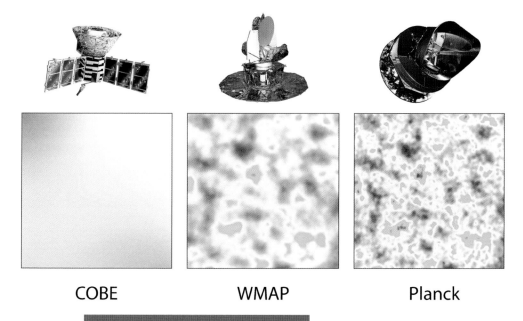

COBE   WMAP   Planck

The measurements of fluctuations in the CMB became increasingly precise with data from WMAP and then Planck.

Conversely, 10^{32} degrees K is 10 with 32 zeroes after it, or 1,000,000,000,000,000,000,000,000,000,000,000 degrees K. The scale of these numbers shows the rapid speed at which the universe was changing and the extreme conditions present in that early period.

As the universe expanded and cooled, the changes began to happen within more comprehensible time scales and environmental conditions.

The First Fractions of a Second

The standard model of big bang cosmology states that the universe began 13.8 billion years ago as a very small, dense region at a temperature of 10^{32} degrees K.

The universe underwent a period of rapid expansion after 10^{-43} seconds, a period known as Planck time. After 10^{-33} seconds, just a short time after it began, the inflation ended and the universe had grown by a factor greater than 10^{35}. Quantum fluctuations that occurred during inflation left very small density fluctuations, or inconsistencies in the composition of the infant universe.

At first the universe was pure energy, but after the big bang, that energy converted into matter. For some reason, that conversion resulted in slightly more matter than matter's counterpart, antimatter. (Antimatter is nearly identical to matter except antimatter particles have the opposite charge and spin of their corresponding matter particles. The two annihilate when they meet.)

The antimatter annihilated with the matter, but for some reason, for every billion antiparticles there were a billion and one particles. As a result, the antimatter was destroyed and some matter remained. The asymmetry between matter and

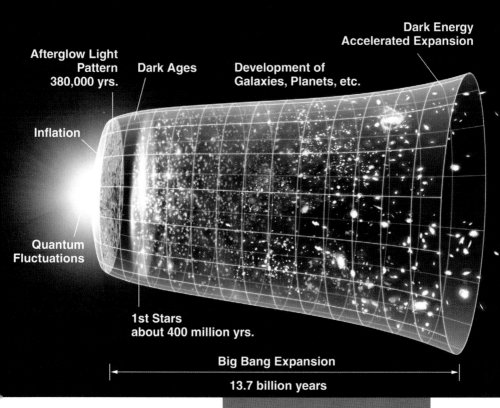

Afterglow Light Pattern 380,000 yrs.

Dark Ages

Development of Galaxies, Planets, etc.

Dark Energy Accelerated Expansion

Inflation

Quantum Fluctuations

1st Stars about 400 million yrs.

Big Bang Expansion

13.7 billion years

This NASA diagram shows the initial rapid expansion of the universe and slower, continued expansion over time.

Dark Matter

Dark matter was first predicted in 1933 by the astronomer Fritz Zwicky. Zwicky discovered that the mass of the stars in the Coma cluster of galaxies accounted for only about 1 percent of the mass necessary to keep the galaxies from escaping the cluster's gravitational pull. Zwicky called this the "missing mass" problem and hypothesized that something else made up the remaining 99 percent.

In the 1970s, astronomers Vera Rubin and W. Kent Ford confirmed that Zwicky's missing mass exists when they measured the mass and speeds of stars in typical galaxies. They found that the mass of the stars in a typical galaxy accounts for just 10 percent of the mass required to keep those stars in orbit around the galactic center. In addition, the stars at the outer edge of a typical galaxy orbit the galactic center just as fast as—or faster than—the stars nearer the center.

Standard physics tells us that if stars at the edge of a spiral galaxy are only experiencing the gravitational effects of the dense galactic center, the stars at the edge of the galaxy should travel slower than stars near the center. Additionally, the visible mass of a galaxy had too little of a gravitational effect to keep the rapidly moving stars in orbit. Rubin and Ford's measurements showed that the galaxies contained a significant amount of unseen mass that accounted for the discrepancies.

Abell 1689, a cluster of galaxies, helps astrophysicists study dark matter because it behaves as a gravitational lens.

Dark matter can also be found by its gravitational lensing effects. Just as the mass of visible objects like the sun distorts space-time and bends light, dark matter bends light passing near it. Today, scientists estimate that 25 to 27 percent of the universe is dark matter, while 5 percent of the universe is **baryonic matter** (ordinary matter made up of protons, neutrons, and atomic nuclei).

antimatter at the beginning of the universe is a mystery to scientists and a topic of current research.

By the first second after the big bang, the universe consisted of a 10-billion-degree K soup of neutrons, protons, electrons, anti-electrons, photons, and neutrinos. At this time, the region of the known universe was at least $10^{19.5}$ cm across.

From Atoms to Stars

The universe cooled for another one hundred seconds and eventually big bang nucleosynthesis convened. In this process, the neutrons and protons formed to create hydrogen nuclei and eventually helium nuclei and traces of other light elements including lithium and beryllium. At this point, there were also about two billion photons per proton or neutron.

After about fifty-six thousand years, the mass density of the universe was equal to the radiation density. At this point in the timeline, the small amounts of density fluctuations mentioned earlier resulted in uneven distribution of dark matter. (Dark matter is a mysterious type of matter that accounts for about 27 percent of the universe.)

Dark matter, though invisible, permeates and shapes the visible universe. The denser regions of dark matter, due to their mass and the effects of gravity, began to attract more dark matter to form dark matter clusters.

After about three hundred thousand years, the universe cooled further and underwent the era of recombination and photon decoupling. This time is the earliest time in the history of the universe that we can directly observe using photons (i.e., via telescopes and other radiation-detecting instruments).

For a very long time, however, there were no other sources of light in the universe. Without stars, there was no visible or infrared light, creating a **cosmic dark ages**.

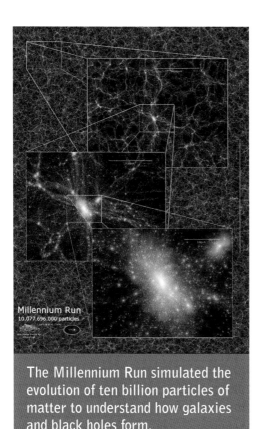

The Millennium Run simulated the evolution of ten billion particles of matter to understand how galaxies and black holes form.

Once neutral atoms were formed, the ordinary matter in the universe began to clump along with the clusters of dark matter due to the dark matter's mass and gravitational pull. As a result, some baryonic regions of the universe were denser than others, and over time these regions attracted more matter. These massive regions eventually collapsed due to gravity and, about two hundred million to three hundred million years after the big bang, formed into stars. The cosmic dark ages ended.

The first stars are thought to have been thirty to three hundred times the size of the sun, likely due to the limited cooling ability of the primordial gas. The minimum mass a clump of gas must have in order to collapse due to gravity is called the **Jeans mass**, which is directly proportional to the square of the gas temperature and inversely proportional to the square root of the gas pressure. The pressure in star-forming regions then was similar to the pressure in star-forming regions today, but the temperature in the densest region of space at this time was between 200 K and 300 K, compared to 10 K in today's star-forming regions. Therefore, the Jeans mass was much higher for the first generation of stars.

The first-generation stars were also millions of times as bright as the sun. They burned through their fuel relatively quickly, fusing elements as heavy as iron within their cores. They died in brilliant supernovas after just a few million years.

In a supernova explosion, the core of a massive star collapses inward and in a fraction of a second, the temperature of the core skyrockets. The resulting explosion produces elements as heavy as uranium and a variety of subatomic particles.

The force of the explosion expels those materials into space, where they become available source material for future stars. When the first stars died in this way, they filled the universe with elements (such as carbon, silicon, and uranium) and particles that would be incorporated into subsequent generations of stars, galaxies, and other celestial objects (thus, the popular sayings by Carl Sagan, "We are made of starstuff" and "If you wish to make an apple pie from scratch, you must first invent the universe").

It is also thought that the supernova death of the earliest stars may have led to the growth of the supermassive black holes that exist today in the hearts of galaxies and power the massive, powerful, energy-emitting quasars.

The second generation of stars had a more complex chemical composition than the first generation of stars and tended to be smaller and longer lived. This is perhaps related to their chemical composition: scientists have found that when a star-forming cloud contains one-thousandth of the metal abundance in the sun or more, those metals help the gas cool and condense more rapidly, which leads to stars of smaller masses and a greater overall rate of star formation.

About one billion years into the universe's timeline, dark matter, stars, and gas clumped together and collapsed under the force of gravity into protogalaxies. Gravity separated each protogalaxy into a core and a halo. The gas particles collided, heated up, radiated energy, and fell into the core while the less interactive dark matter remained in the halo. The protogalaxies became increasingly dense, and stars began to form, turning the first protogalaxies into full, primeval galaxies.

The first galaxies eventually formed into galaxy clusters and sometimes collided and merged with other galaxies. Over time, the universe expanded to be at least 10^{29} cm across at a temperature of 2.725 degrees K. Earth-like planets formed around the second-generation stars, and life on Earth began about four billion years ago.

Today, we can study as far back as the era of recombination because we can look back in history by looking farther across the universe. As the universe expands and light from increasingly distant galaxies reaches Earth, astronomers and physicists get a look not just into the distance but into the

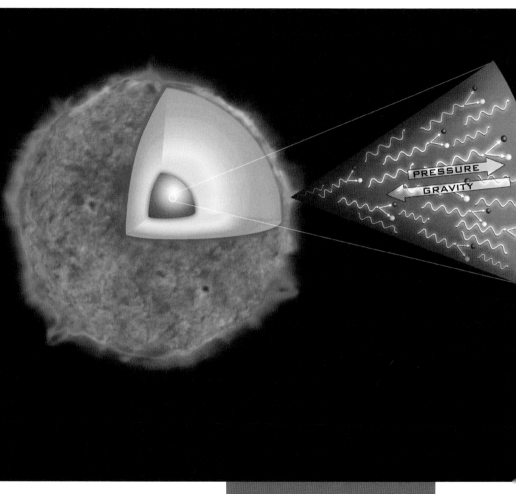

As a star runs out of fuel, the core becomes so heavy that the star collapses under its own gravitational force.

distant past. Because of the vast amount of space between us and the edge of the observable universe, the light that reaches us from that edge has traveled billions of years to reach us. In doing so, it gives us a peek into what the universe was like billions of years ago.

In the last century, many pieces of the cosmological puzzle have come together. Through the work of many physicists, astronomers, and astrophysicists, we have a huge amount of knowledge and new technologies that are useful in space and on Earth. However, many mysteries still elude scientists. How did the laws of physics operate in those intense, initial conditions? How did matter come to prevail over antimatter? We'll go over these questions in the next chapter.

The ATLAS detector at CERN is used
for a wide range of physics experiments,
such as searching for extra dimensions.

CHAPTER 5

The Big Bang Theory's Influence Today

The big bang may have taken place almost fourteen billion years ago, but as a society, we're far from past it. The big bang theory is the standard model taught in astronomy and cosmology courses around the world. Significant funding and research time is dedicated to understanding more about the big bang and filling in the remaining questions in the cosmological model.

PARTICLE ACCELERATORS

It's currently impossible to look back past the time of recombination (the moment when free electrons paired up with nuclei to form neutral atoms and photons of light were finally able to travel freely) with telescopes. That means the first four hundred thousand years or so of the universe can be studied only indirectly, such as by observing and analyzing the cosmic microwave background radiation for clues to the early universe or by re-creating the conditions of the big bang.

Physicists use particle accelerators to reproduce those incredibly hot, incredibly dense early conditions of the universe. Particle accelerators are powerful instruments that produce and accelerate a beam of particles, typically protons or electrons, but occasionally entire atoms such as gold or uranium. The particles are accelerated inside a beam pipe to greater and greater energies. When the particles have reached the desired energy levels, they are collided with another beam or a fixed target, such as a thin piece of metal.

The collision produces a shower of exotic particles. Detectors record the particles and the paths they take after the collision, which gives physicists a wealth of data to sort through in the aftermath.

The most famous particle accelerator studying the early conditions of the universe is the Large Hadron Collider, which is buried underground along the French and Swiss border at CERN (the European Organization for Nuclear Research). The Large Hadron Collider (LHC) is also the world's largest particle accelerator with a ring 17 miles (27 km) long.

The LHC has four detectors at different collision points on the ring that physicists use for different purposes. ATLAS is a general purpose detector designed to investigate new physics, such as searching for extra dimensions and dark matter. CMS looks for similar things as ATLAS using different technology. ALICE is a heavy ion detector used to study the physics of strongly interacting matter at extreme energy densities similar to those just after the big bang. LHCb investigates the differences between matter and antimatter.

In one recent experiment, the scientists at CERN used the ALICE detector to study the collision of heavy ions (such as gold and lead nuclei) at energies of a few trillion electron volts each. The resulting collision, which CERN described as a "miniscule fireball," re-created the hot, dense soup of particles moving at extremely high energies in the early universe.

The particle mixture was primarily made up subatomic particles called quarks and gluons that moved freely. (Quarks are particles that make up matter; gluons carry the strong force that binds quarks together.) For just a few millionths of

The quark-gluon plasma existed for a few microseconds after the universe began before cooling and condensing to form protons and neutrons.

a second after the big bang, the bonds between quarks and gluons were weak and the two types of particles were able to move freely in what's known as a quark-gluon plasma.

The LHC's man-made fireball cooled immediately, and the individual quarks and gluons recombined and created many different types of particles, from protons, neutrons, antiprotons, and antineutrons to tiny particles called pions and kaons. One early finding from analysis of the quark-gluon plasma showed scientists that the plasma behaves more like a fluid than a gas, contrary to many researchers' expectations.

Scientists at CERN are also using the Large Hadron Collider's LHCb detector to determine what caused the imbalance between matter and antimatter after the big bang.

Other Uses for Accelerators

Particle accelerators were invented by experimental physicists to study particle physics, but they have since been used in many useful applications.

From Splitting the Atom to the Atomic Bomb

The first particle accelerator was built in 1929 by John Cockcroft and Ernest Walton in pursuit of splitting the atom to study the nucleus. They succeeded in 1932 when they bombarded lithium with high-energy hydrogen protons. Their experiment was the first time humans split an atom, a process called fission.

The experiment also confirmed Einstein's law $E=mc^2$. Walton and Cockcroft found that their experiment produced two atoms of helium plus energy. The mass of the helium nuclei was slightly less than the mass of the combined lithium and hydrogen nuclei, but the loss in mass was accounted for by the amount of energy released.

In 1939, German physicists discovered how to split a uranium atom. Scientists across the world feared that the Nazis would build an atomic bomb capable of terrible destruction. (When the uranium-235 isotope is split, the fission begins a chain reaction that can grow large enough to cause an enormous explosion.) At the urging of Einstein and other top physicists, in 1941 the United States government launched an atomic bomb development effort code-named the Manhattan Project.

Over 120,000 Americans worked on the Manhattan Project, and the government spent almost $2 billion on research and development. The effort was so top secret that Vice President Harry

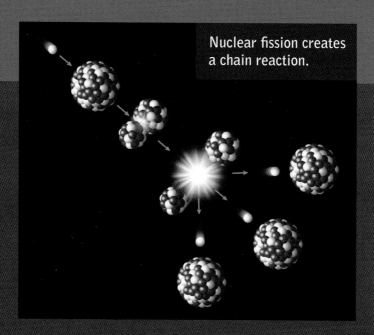

Nuclear fission creates a chain reaction.

Truman didn't learn about the Manhattan Project until President Theodore Roosevelt died in office and Truman became president.

When Japan refused to surrender in 1945, Truman authorized two atomic bombs that were dropped on Hiroshima and Nagasaki on August 6 and August 9, respectively. The bombs effectively ended World War II, but hundreds of thousands of Japanese people were killed and many more suffered terrible health effects from the radiation.

For example, particle accelerators are used to deliver radiation therapy, which is one of the standard methods for treating cancer. In one form, high energy X-rays are generated by beaming high-energy electrons at a material such as tungsten. These X-rays are then directed at the site of the patient's cancerous tumor to kill the cancer cells. Healthy tissue is also damaged by the radiation beam, however, and researchers are continually looking for ways to deliver the right dose of radiation to destroy the tumor while minimizing impact to healthy cells.

Particle accelerators are also used to generate X-rays for medical imaging, such as when we have our teeth X-rayed at the dentist's office or have a full-body magnetic resonance imaging (MRI) scan.

Outside of the medical world, particle accelerators are used for industrial purposes, such as manufacturing computer chips and producing the plastic used in shrink-wrap, for security purposes, such as inspecting cargo, and in many other applications.

UNSOLVED QUESTIONS

Physicists are able to study many aspects of the big bang using particle accelerators, but their work is by no means over. There are still many enormous questions about the beginning of the universe. The major questions include:

- How did all four forces combine in the first fraction of a second?
- What gave particles their mass?
- Why did particles outnumber antiparticles?
- How can we detect and study the neutrinos believed to have been created in the big bang, and what will they tell us if we find them?

- How can we detect and study the **gravitational waves** that are believed to have been created by the big bang?
- Is our universe the only universe?

The Four Forces

The Standard Model of particle physics has been developed since the 1930s, with significant help from particle accelerators and their cataclysmic investigations into atoms and their component parts.

According to the Standard Model, everything in the universe is made of a few fundamental particles (such as the building blocks of matter, quarks and leptons), governed by four fundamental forces (the gravitational, electromagnetic, weak, and strong forces). The Standard Model explains how these particles and three of the forces relate to one another.

The electromagnetic force, which governs the propagation of light and the magnetism that allows a magnet to pick up a paper clip, reaches over great distances, as evidenced by starlight reaching Earth. The weak force governs beta decay (a form of natural radioactivity) and hydrogen fusion and acts at distances smaller than the atomic nucleus. The strong force holds together the nucleus and acts at very small distances.

The electromagnetic, weak, and strong forces result from the exchange of a force-carrying particle that belongs to a larger group of particles called bosons. Each force has its own boson: the strong force is carried by the gluon, the electromagnetic force is carried by the photon, and the weak force is carried by W and Z bosons.

The Standard Model is able to explain the forces other than gravity, all of which operate on microscopic scales. Gravity, however, operates across large distances, and as of yet, there is only a theoretical boson called the gravitron that corresponds to the gravitational force. Even without gravity, however, the Standard Model is able to explain particle physics very well because the gravitational force has little effect at the small scale of particles.

Research has shown that at very high energies, the electromagnetic and weak forces unite into a single force. Scientists believe that at even higher energies the strong force converges with the electroweak force to create a grand unified theory (GUT).

It is thought that at the extreme conditions immediately after the big bang all four forces would have been unified, but scientists do not yet understand how this could work. (Einstein died working to discover the unified field theory, continuing his work even on his deathbed.) Figuring out this unified force could help scientists understand more about the big bang and where our universe came from.

The Higgs Boson

The big bang created intense amounts of radiation, which has no mass. Eventually, the radiation converted into matter, which does have mass. Where did this mass come from?

On July 4, 2012, scientists at CERN discovered a new particle called the Higgs boson. The Higgs boson is a particle that belongs to an invisible field called the Higgs field that pervades the universe. Higgs bosons are denser spots in the Higgs field that can be detected in particle accelerators.

The Higgs field theory, proposed in 1964 by British physicist Peter Higgs, as well as by François Englert and Robert Brout, explains how particles gain mass. The theory states that when a particle moves through the Higgs field, a small amount of distortion (as if something was being dragged, creating resistance) is created that gives the particle mass. The more a particle interacts with the field, the more mass it acquires.

Other particles don't interact with the Higgs field at all and have no mass.

One analogy that is commonly used to illustrate the effect of the Higgs field is to imagine a large party filled with people. When an accountant (stereotypically a dull job) walks through the room, nobody interacts with the accountant, much like certain particles such as photons don't interact with the Higgs field. The accountant (and the photon) move freely.

On the other hand, what if a celebrity walks through the party? People near the door see the celebrity first and begin spreading the news to their neighbors, and the news spreads through the crowd. The crowd converges on the celebrity, slowing down her progression through the crowd.

The celebrity has become a massive particle through her interaction with the crowd. The Higgs boson can be thought of as a dense clump in the crowd created by an exciting piece of gossip, and as the gossip spreads through the crowd, the clump moves through the crowd.

The Higgs boson had been a cornerstone of the Standard Model of particle physics since the 1970s, but the 2012 discovery at CERN gave significant support to its existence.

More recently, CERN physicists have determined the mass of the Higgs boson and measured other characteristics. Active research into the Higgs boson and Higgs field is still underway as there is still much to discover.

Matter Versus Antimatter

Matter and antimatter particles are created in pairs, which means that the big bang should have created equal amounts of matter and antimatter. Matter and antimatter annihilate one another upon contact, and in the first fractions of a second, the universe was filled with particle and antiparticle pairs popping in and out of existence. At the end of this process, when all the annihilations were complete, the universe should have been filled with pure energy—and nothing else.

This is clearly not the case. We are made of matter, and we inhabit a world and universe made of matter. What, then, happened such that matter survived?

Scientists calculate that about one particle per billion particles of matter survived. It's unknown why this is the case, but observations of particles at the LHC give one potential explanation:

Due to a weak interaction process, particles can oscillate between their particle and antiparticle state before decaying into other particles of matter or antimatter. It could be that in the early universe an unknown mechanism caused oscillating particles to decay into matter slightly more often than they decayed into antimatter.

The survival of matter over antimatter is a topic of ongoing investigation at physics institutions across the world.

Big Bang Neutrinos

Scientists across the world are searching for big bang neutrinos in hopes that these ancient particles could reveal more about the early universe.

Neutrinos were first hypothesized in 1930 by Wolfgang Pauli as particles that carried away the observed difference in energy between the initial particles and final particles when a neutron decayed into a proton and an electron. The first neutrino was detected twenty-six years later.

Neutrinos are a fundamental, subatomic particle produced by the decay of radioactive elements. They're produced within particle accelerators, nuclear power stations, nuclear bombs, stars, and the big bang itself. Neutrinos have no electric charge and are therefore not affected by the electromagnetic force. They hardly interact with anything, in fact, which allows neutrinos to move easily through matter and across the

There are five thousand of these optical detectors buried in the ice at the South Pole, ready to detect neutrino collisions.

universe without interference. (Nearly one hundred trillion neutrinos zip through your body every second!)

Neutrinos are extremely desirable particles to study because they travel largely unaffected across space and bring information to us from deep within the cosmos. A strongly interacting particle, in contrast, would be absorbed by the matter and radiation in between. But because neutrinos are so weakly interacting, they are also very hard to detect. Therefore, neutrino detectors must be very large in order to maximize the chance that a passing neutrino will interact. They are typically built inside of transparent material such as water so the instruments can detect the light given off by particles produced by neutrino interactions.

The world's largest neutrino detector is Ice Cube, buried within a cubic kilometer of ultra-transparent ice in Antarctica. The detectors are buried about .9 miles (1,500 m) beneath the surface of the ice to shield them from the radiation at Earth's surface. When a neutrino collides with a molecule of ice, the collision will create an array of subatomic particles and give off light, which is picked up by Ice Cube's detectors.

While detectors like Ice Cube have detected neutrinos from cosmic sources, no detector yet has picked up big bang neutrinos. These ancient particles are predicted to be billions of times colder than neutrinos from the sun, and their collisions would be much less energetic.

One experiment dedicated to detecting just these cold relic neutrinos is a prototype lab, PTOLEMY, at the US Department of Energy's Princeton Plasma Physics Laboratory. PTOLEMY's instruments were designed to have the coldest, darkest conditions possible so that the tiny amount of energy that a big bang neutrino contains can, upon collision, stand out and be observed.

The PTOLEMY scientists hope to show that they can measure the mass of a big bang neutrino and then ramp up from a prototype laboratory to a full lab that can uncover even more information from big bang neutrinos.

Gravitational Waves

Scientists believe that the initial cosmic inflation should have magnified quantum fluctuations in the early universe's gravitational field, resulting in gravitational waves.

Gravitational waves were first predicted by Albert Einstein in his 1915 general theory of relativity. Gravitational waves, from the collision of two black holes, were first detected by LIGO (the Laser Interferometer Gravitational-Wave Observatory) in 2015.

The gravitational waves LIGO picked up confirmed Einstein's prediction and also showed that black holes do collide. However, scientists are still on the hunt for gravitational waves specifically from cosmic inflation. Inflation-caused gravitational waves would be too weak for the LIGO detector to pick up, but they would slightly twist the orientation of light, creating an effect called polarization.

In 2012, a group behind the BICEP2 radio telescope at the South Pole thought they had detected big bang gravitational waves. Their data had shown a curlicue pattern in the polarization of the CMB, which greatly excited the science community and made news headlines around the world. However, the pattern turned out to be from dust in the Milky Way, which emits polarized light with the same curling pattern.

Research is still underway using an upgraded version of the original technology called BICEP3 whose observation period ran through much of 2016. BICEP3 includes more detectors and a finer resolution but also a broader spectrum of light that will help the team discern any signals from inflation from galactic dust.

The Multiverse

One of the major questions around the history of our universe is whether our universe is the sole universe. Are there other universes that have undergone a similar cosmology? Are there other universes that have undergone very different cosmologies?

If you currently have a basic assumption that our universe is the only universe, it can be challenging to imagine what it means for other universes to exist. But at one time, people thought our planet was the only planet, and then that the sun was the only sun, and then that our galaxy was the only galaxy. One by one, these notions have been shattered by theoretical and observational science. It follows that we should then seriously consider whether our universe is the only universe or if it is one of many.

According to Brian Greene, one of the most prominent theoretical physicists who studies and speaks on the idea of multiple universes:

An illustration of the gravitational waves (disruptions in space-time) caused by two black holes orbiting one another

What we have found in research ... is that our mathematical investigations are suggesting that what we have thought to be everything may actually be a tiny part of a much grander cosmos. And that grander cosmos can contain other realms that seem to rightly be called universe just as our realm has been called universe.

One relatively simple example Greene gives begins by considering whether the universe is finite or infinite. Currently, physicists do not know which is true. Thus, an infinite universe can be considered a viable option.

Next, consider shuffling a deck of cards an infinite number of times. Eventually, the order of the cards will begin to repeat. So, too, would the configuration of particles in an infinite universe. If space goes on for infinity, there would inevitably be repeating configurations of matter just as there are repeating configurations of cards.

While these other universes have not yet been observed, there have been other successful theories that started in a similar way. Einstein's general theory of relativity, for example, started as a theoretical set of equations and was later tested in various ways before becoming a well-supported, accepted theory.

The collection of multiple universes is called a **multiverse**. It is also sometimes called a bubble universe because the term describes how physicists imagine multiple universes forming.

To imagine a bubble universe, picture a boiling pot of water. The pot has bubbles of varying sizes. Some appear and pop immediately, others grow larger and last longer. (This is not to say that the energy fueling a multiverse is thermal energy, but the image is helpful for imagining the appearance and disappearance of universes with varying sizes and lifespans.)

In this model, our region of space underwent its early cosmic expansion, which ended 13.8 billion years ago. While inflation in our region ended, inflation continued in other regions or "bubbles." The different inflation regions separated, creating an infinite number of universes. As they inflate, the bubbles grow apart and make room for more inflating bubbles.

The idea of a multiverse or bubble universe is controversial, in part because initially scientists had no way to prove or disprove that a multiverse exists. A core component of the scientific method is the ability to test a hypothesis, and without that component, a hypothesis essentially becomes a question of philosophy, not of science.

van Ravenswaay

Scientists are looking for impact marks that could show other universes have collided with ours. These marks would validate the multiverse theory.

However, in recent years, astrophysicists have thought of a way to test the multiverse theory. Consider again the pot of boiling water analogy—as water boils, some of the bubbles that rise up will collide. We don't know how dense the theoretical multiverse would be, but it is possible that another universe could have collided with our own.

Astrophysicists think that such a collision would be observable as imprints or "bruises" on the cosmic microwave background. The collision point would be a round spot of either higher or lower radiation intensity. While it's not a guarantee that our (hypothetical) bubble universe has collided with another bubble universe, finding such an imprint would lend significant support to the multiverse theory.

String Theory

The idea of a multiverse is especially attractive for proponents of **string theory**. String theory is a theory that attempts to integrate general relativity with quantum mechanics.

In string theory, the fundamental components of all matter are tiny strings that vibrate in eleven dimensions. Just like a guitar string can vibrate in different ways that produce different notes, in string theory, strings have different "excitation modes," or frequencies that produce different particles. If string theory is accurate, it explains not just the subatomic particle but also the laws of physics.

String theory is a complex theory beyond the scope of this book, but it's worth noting briefly for two major reasons: string theory is one possible way to achieve a unified theory of physics. More significantly for the multiverse theory, string theory is another one of the mathematical models that predicts that there may be many different universes.

OPPONENTS of the BIG BANG THEORY

The big bang theory, like most scientific theories, has its opponents. While most of the opposition comes from the realm of religious people who favor a literal interpretation of their religious texts, there have been small camps of scientists who held out against the big bang model of cosmology into the twentieth century.

Scientific Opposition

The big bang theory of cosmology is the standard model accepted by a majority of scientists. However, the steady state theorist Fred Hoyle continued to oppose the big bang theory throughout his life, as did his *Synthesis of the Elements in Stars* coauthors Margaret and Geoffrey Burbidge.

Geoffrey Burbidge created a revision of the steady state theory called the "quasi-Steady State." The new version of the theory proposes that the universe expands and contracts over one-hundred-billion-year cycles. According to the Burbidges, if stars can eject new types of matter as their paper with Hoyle showed, perhaps galaxies could also eject huge collections of matter to create new galaxies. Margaret Burbidge spent years observing quasars, theorizing that they could be a candidate for these ejected collections of matter.

In a 2005 interview with *Discover* magazine, Geoffrey Burbidge said:

> The present situation in cosmology is that most people like to believe they know what the skeleton looks like, and they're putting flesh on the bones. And Fred [Hoyle] and I would continuously say, we don't even know what the skeleton looks like. We don't know whether it's got 20 heads instead of one, or 60 arms or legs. It's probable that the universe we live in is not the way I think it is or the way the Big Bang people think it is. In 200 years, somebody is going to say how stupid we were.

In other words, Burbidge believes that too many scientists have prematurely accepted the current big bang model of cosmology. Geoffrey Burbidge has since died, and Margaret Burbidge is in her late nineties. Few other scientists have continued to oppose the big bang theory.

Religious Opposition

The predominant opposition to the big bang comes from those who disagree due to religious reasons. The Institute for Creation Research, which bills itself as a "leader in scientific research within the context of biblical creation," publishes articles such as "The Big Bang Theory Collapses" that characterize the big bang theory as irreparably flawed—though scientific studies show otherwise. The ICR ultimately argues against any scientific cosmology, including the quasi-steady state model, because they all contradict the ICR's belief that the Christian god created heaven and Earth.

The ICR is just one example of literal religious thinkers who oppose the big bang theory. There are many others who dismiss the model for similar reasons.

There are also many religious people who do not dismiss the big bang theory. Georges Lemaître was himself a Catholic priest, and many religious thinkers from various faiths see no opposition between the big bang model of cosmology and their religious beliefs. Some see their creator as the creative force that sparked the big bang, while others, as Lemaître, consider the religious and scientific realms as entirely separate and able to exist separately without conflict.

CONCLUSION

Many of the major questions that exist about the big bang model of cosmology—such as what came before the big bang, do other universes exist, and how did the fundamental forces unite in those first fractions of a second—are simply curiosities to many people outside of the science world. And yet, the answers, when we find them, will fundamentally shape the way we understand how we came to be where we are today. Few questions matter more.

Chronology

13.8 billion years ago   Our universe begins with a big bang followed by cosmic inflation; light elements form within first three seconds

13.76 billion years ago   Recombination takes place, and light can travel freely through the universe; the cosmic dark ages begin

13.57 billion years ago   The first stars form, ending the cosmic dark ages

5 billion years ago   The sun is born

3.8 billion years ago   Earliest life-forms appear on Earth

13th century   Glass lenses developed

1543   Nicolaus Copernicus publishes *On the Revolutions of the Heavenly Spheres* with his heliocentric theory of the solar system

1572   Tycho Brahe observes a supernova, which shows that changes do happen in the celestial realm

1577	Brahe observes a comet and calculates that it had passed by Venus, another crack in the Aristotelian model of unchanging, crystalline spheres
1608	First two patents are filed for telescope designs, both by spectacle makers in the Netherlands
1609	Galileo Galilei builds a telescope and begins observing the sky; Johannes Kepler publishes his first two laws of planetary motion
1610	Galileo discovers Jupiter's four largest moons and the phases of Venus
1633	Galileo is found guilty of heresy for supporting the heliocentric model of the universe and sentenced to house arrest for the rest of his life
1665	Sir Isaac Newton shows that white light contains all of the colors of the rainbow
1668	Newton builds the first reflecting telescope
1676	Ole Römer measures the speed of light
1800	Sir William Herschel discovers infrared light
1911	Ernest Rutherford discovers the atomic nucleus
1915	Albert Einstein publishes his general theory of relativity

1924	Edwin Hubble discovers that other galaxies exist outside of the Milky Way
1927	Georges Lemaître publishes his first paper on an expanding universe
1929	Hubble discovers that galaxies are receding at speeds directly correlated to their distance
1931	Lemaître publishes an article in the journal *Nature* with his theory of the "primeval atom"
1948	George Gamow and Ralph Alpher publish "On the Origin of Chemical Elements" theorizing how elements are formed from the big bang
1957	Fred Hoyle and three colleagues publish "Synthesis of the Elements in Stars" showing how the heavier elements are formed
1965	Arno Penzias and Robert Wilson discover the cosmic microwave background radiation
1989	George Smoot's team launches the COBE satellite to study the CMB for the seeds of galaxies
1992	Smoot announces that COBE's data showed small fluctuations in the CMB

Glossary

antimatter Antimatter is nearly identical to matter except antimatter particles have the opposite charge and spin of their corresponding matter particles.

apparent brightness How bright a star looks to an observer.

baryonic matter Ordinary matter made up of protons, neutrons, and atomic nuclei.

big bang nucleosynthesis The formation of light nuclei immediately after the big bang, including helium, deuterium, lithium, and beryllium.

blueshift The shift of a galaxy's or other object's emitted light toward bluer (shorter) wavelengths due to its radial velocity toward Earth.

comet A cosmic object made of ice, rock, and dust that orbits the sun. When near the sun, some of the ice sublimates and produces a luminous tail.

cosmic dark ages The several hundred million years between recombination and the appearance of the first stars during which the universe was completely dark and devoid of observable data.

cosmology The science of the origin and evolution of the universe.

dark matter A mysterious type of matter that accounts for about 27 percent of the universe.

electromagnetic spectrum The entire range of wavelengths or frequencies of radiation, from gamma rays to radio waves.

European Renaissance The flourishing of European civilization immediately after the Middle Ages, including in scholarship, commerce, exploration, and innovation.

gravitational waves Ripples in space-time that result from violent and energetic processes in the universe, such as the collision of two black holes or the big bang itself.

Hubble constant The rate at which the universe is expanding, estimated to be somewhere between 45 kilometers per second per megaparsec to 90 kilometers per second per megaparsec.

incandescence The emission of visible light from an object heated to high temperatures.

infrared light Radiation with a wavelength just longer than the red end of the visible light spectrum but shorter than the microwave portion of the electromagnetic spectrum.

Jeans mass The minimum mass a clump of gas in outer space must have in order to collapse due to gravity.

luminosity The total amount of energy a star radiates in all directions each second; the absolute brightness of a star.

megaparsec A measurement of distance used in astronomy; one parsec is 3.26 light-years long, and one megaparsec (Mpc) is 3.26 million light-years long.

multiverse A theoretical set of universes in which our universe is just one of many.

nebulae Clouds of gas and dust in outer space. Before Edwin Hubble's discovery of the Andromeda galaxy, scientists thought all other galaxies were nebula inside the Milky Way.

parallax The difference in an object's apparent position when viewed from two different lines of sight.

period In astronomy, the frequency at which a variable star pulsates.

photon Tiny fundamental particles of electromagnetic radiation.

photon decoupling The separation of photons from baryons (particles of ordinary matter); the point about 380,000 years after the big bang at which photons began to travel freely.

quanta A discrete quantity of energy, such as a quanta of light. Quanta were first theorized by Max Planck, who proposed that all energy at the subatomic level can only be transferred in discrete (not continuous) amounts.

quantum mechanics The branch of physics that describes the motion and interaction of matter and light on the atomic and subatomic scale.

recombination The time in which electrons and atomic nuclei combined to form neutral atoms.

redshift The shift of a galaxy's or other object's emitted light toward redder (longer) wavelengths due to the expansion of the universe and growing distance between objects in space.

Scientific Revolution The period between the sixteenth and eighteenth centuries in the Western world in which science and technology advanced at a rapid pace with many important discoveries.

steady state The alternative model of cosmology that holds that the universe is infinite and constantly expanding but, because matter is being continuously created, maintains constant density.

stellar nucleosynthesis The formation of nuclei inside of stars, a process responsible for the elements heavier than helium.

string theory A theoretical framework that suggests the fundamental building blocks of matter are tiny vibrating strings.

supernova The highly energetic explosion of a massive star at the end of its lifecycle.

ultraviolet light Radiation with a wavelength just shorter than the blue end of the visible light spectrum but longer than the wavelength of the X-ray portion of the electromagnetic spectrum.

wave-particle duality The nature of light and matter to have characteristics of both particles (such as discrete amounts of energy) and waves (such as wavelength and frequency).

Further Information

BOOKS

Carroll, Sean. *The Particle at the End of the Universe.* New York: Penguin Group, 2012.

deGrasse Tyson, Neil, and Donald Goldsmith. *Origins: Fourteen Billion Years of Cosmic Evolution.* New York: W.W. Norton & Co., 2004.

Singh, Simon. *Big Bang: The Origin of the Universe.* New York: HarperCollins Publishers Inc., 2004.

WEBSITES

Cosmology Interactive
http://highered.mheducation.com/sites/007299181x/student_view0/chapter26/cosmology_interactive.html#

Tweak the conditions of the universe, specifically the Hubble constant and the density of the universe, and see how your altered big bang cosmology unfolds.

Mysteries of Deep Space Interactive Timeline
http://www.pbs.org/deepspace/timeline/

Explore the universe's history using this interactive timeline to learn more about the first fractions of a second all the way up to the projected end of the universe.

Take a Trip Through the Big Bang
http://www.superstringtheory.com/cosmo/cosmo3.html

Take a tour of the early universe, with illustrations that bring radiation and particle interactions to life.

VIDEOS

"Is Our Universe the Only Universe?"
https://www.ted.com/talks/brian_greene_why_is_our_
universe_fine_tuned_for_life?language=en

In this TED Talk, Brian Greene discusses how exploring the big bang and cosmic inflation has led to the theory of a multiverse.

"Where Did the Universe Come From?"
https://www.quantamagazine.org/20150612-in-theory-cosmic-
inflation/

Theoretical particle physicist David Kaplan discusses cosmic inflation and the origin of the universe.

Bibliography

Alpher, R. A., H. Bethe, and G. Gamow. "The Origin of Chemical Elements." *Physical Review* 73 no. 7 (1948): 803–804.

Becker, Kate. "Gravitational Waves from Bubble Universe Collisions?" PBS. Retrieved October 24, 2016. http://www.pbs.org/wgbh/nova/blogs/physics/2015/05/a-new-way-to-detect-bubble-universe-collisions.

CERN. "Heavy Ions and Quark-Gluon Plasma." Retrieved October 24, 2016. https://home.cern/about/physics/heavy-ions-and-quark-gluon-plasma.

Christianson, J. R., and Tycho Brahe. "Tycho Brahe's German Treatise on the Comet of 1577: A Study in Science and Politics." *Isis* 70 no. 1 (1979): 110–140.

Galilei, Galileo. "Siderus Nuncius," trans. Edward Stafford Carlos, ed. Peter Barker. Retrieved October 24, 2016. http://homepages.wmich.edu/~mcgrew/Siderius.pdf.

Gallart, Sílvia Bravo. "Why Neutrinos Matter." TED-Ed, April 28, 2015. https://www.youtube.com/watch?v=nkydJXigkRE.

Greene, Brian, interviewed by Amir D. Aczel. "Dr. Brian Greene String Theory, The Multiverse and more." *The Hidden Reality*, March 2, 2011. https://www.youtube.com/watch?v=GbFg1ocDOMk.

IceCube. "All About Neutrinos." Retrieved October 24, 2016. https://icecube.wisc.edu/info/neutrinos.

Isaacson, Walter. *Einstein: His Life and Universe.* New York, NY: Simon and Schuster, 2007.

Larson, Richard B., and Volker Bromm. "The First Stars in the Universe." *Scientific American*, January 19, 2009. https://www.scientificamerican.com/article/the-first-stars-in-the-un/.

Lemaître, Georges. "A Homogenous Universe of Constant Mass and Increasing Radius Accounting for the Radial Velocity of Extra-Galactic Nebulae." *Monthly Notices of the Royal Astronomical Society* 91 (1931): 483–490.

———. "The Beginning of the World from the Point of View of Quantum Theory." *Nature* 127 (1931): 706.

———. "The Expanding Universe." *Monthly Notices of the Royal Astronomical Society* 91 (1931): 490–501.

Lincoln, Don. "The Higgs Field Explained." Ted-Ed, August 27, 2013. https://www.youtube.com/watch?v=joTKd5j3mzk/.

McLintock, A.H., ed. "Maori Myths and Traditions." *An Encyclopaedia of New Zealand.* Wellington, New Zealand: R.E. Owen, Government Printer: 1966.

Nobelprize.org. "Arno Penzias—Biographical." 2014. http://
www.nobelprize.org/nobel_prizes/physics/laureates/1978/
penzias-bio.html

———. "George Smoot—Biographical." 2014. https://www.
nobelprize.org/nobel_prizes/physics/laureates/2006/smoot-
bio.html.

———. "Robert Woodrow Wilson—Biographical." 2014.
http://www.nobelprize.org/nobel_prizes/physics/
laureates/1978/wilson-bio.html.

Panek, Richard, and Catherine Ledner. "Two Against the
Big Bang." *Discover Magazine* (November 2005). http://
discovermagazine.com/2005/nov/two-against-the-big-bang.

Singh, Simon. *Big Bang: The Origin of the Universe.* New York,
NY: HarperCollins Publishers Inc., 2004.

Vilenkin, Alexander, and Max Tegmark. "The Case for Parallel
Universes." *Scientific American,* July 19, 2011. https://www.
scientificamerican.com/article/multiverse-the-case-for-
parallel-universe/.

Weinberg, Steven. *The First Three Minutes.* New York, NY:
Basic Books: 1993.

Witzel, Michael. *The Origins of the World's Mythologies.* New
York, NY: Oxford University Press, 2012.

About the Author

Rachel Keranen is a writer based in Madison, Wisconsin. Her work focuses on science, software, and entrepreneurship. She's passionate about learning and loves taking deep dives into science and history. In addition to the books that she writes for Cavendish Square, such as *Evolution* and *The Composition of the Universe: The Evolution of Stars and Galaxies*, Keranen's previous work includes articles in the *Minneapolis/St. Paul Business Journal* and *London Business Matters* magazine.

Keranen enjoys traveling, biking, and spending time near water. As a young girl, her parents often pulled her out of bed in the middle of the night to watch shooting stars and meteor showers.

WITHDRAWN
Anne Arundel Co. Public Library